Undiscovered Horizons

The Ultimate Destination of Life's Most Incredible Odyssey

James A. McComb

Order this book online at www.trafford.com
or email orders@trafford.com

Most Trafford titles are also available at major online book retailers.

© Copyright 2013 James A. McComb.

All rights reserved. No part of this publication may be reproduced, stored in a retrieval system, or transmitted, in any form or by any means, electronic, mechanical, photocopying, recording, or otherwise, without the written prior permission of the author.

Scripture notations marked (NLT) are taken from the Holy Bible, New Living Translation, copyright © 1996, 2004, 2007 by Tyndale House Foundation. Used by permission of Tyndale House Publishers, Inc., Carol Stream, Illinois 60188. All rights reserved.

Printed in the United States of America.

ISBN: 978-1-4251-4029-8 (sc)
ISBN: 978-1-4669-9513-0 (hc)
ISBN: 978-1-4669-9512-3 (e)

Trafford rev. 05/22/2013

 www.trafford.com

North America & international
toll-free: 1 888 232 4444 (USA & Canada)
phone: 250 383 6864 ♦ fax: 812 355 4082

Contents

Preface ix
Acknowledgements xv

1	Life: It's No Accident	1
2	Undiscovered Horizons	17
3	Rules of the Road	37
4	The Five Keys	55
5	Direction: The First Key	61
6	Attraction: The Second Key	73
7	Opportunity: The Third Key	85
8	Inspiration: The Fourth Key	95
9	Inherence: The Fifth Key	107
10	Horizon: Discovered	115
11	The Power in You	125
12	Life's Most Incredible Odyssey	137
13	The Ultimate Destination	147

Appendix A: Life Mission 159
Appendix B: Vision 163
Appendix C: Success Measures 175
Appendix D: Strategies 179
Appendix E: Tactics 185
Appendix F: Evaluating Progress 189

In Loving Dedication

Miss Josephine Mathews, my English teacher at Roosevelt Junior High in Rockford, Illinois from 1966-1969. She was God's hand, leading me toward my purpose, even before I knew I had one.

Janice Laureen, Executive Director of the Association for Strategic Planning, based in Los Angeles. She was my good friend and cheerleader while I wrote this book, and passed away a year before it was finished.

Steve Haines, CEO of the worldwide Haines Centre for Strategic Management, based in San Diego. He was my mentor, in business and in life, and passed away a few months before this book was published.

Gary McDonald, CEO of C & G Marketing in Portland, Oregon. A man of tremendous courage and wisdom, he has been one of my most cherished friends for more than 23 years.

Sally Barilone McComb, my wife since October 16, 2010. She is my soul mate, and fellow traveler on the road to our Undiscovered Horizons.

Preface

*Life's most incredible odyssey
is the journey to fulfill your own unique Personal Destiny.
But if you never make that journey,
you miss the very essence of the Life you were born to live.*

Jim McComb (1954-present)
Author, keynote speaker, ordinary guy

I wrote this book, quite simply, because I was called to do it.

Now, when you hear me say I was "called" to do it, your mind no doubt conjures up some epic Hollywood moment of McComb ascending to the mountaintop to receive stone tablets containing the copy for this book directly from the hand of God Himself. Well, before you begin chuckling to yourself and dismissing me as delightfully delusional, please know that it didn't exactly happen that way. In fact, the process was actually excruciatingly slow and God's hand in it was largely invisible to me until about two years before this book was published.

It has taken me eight years to write, and re-write, this book. The themes in it have been bouncing around in my head for a long time, but I was never certain why they were there. I just *knew* that my thoughts would be of value to *someone* and I felt *compelled* to write about them. But I never seemed to have enough time or—strangely—enough motivation either. That created problems for me when I began this challenging undertaking eight years ago, because I actually *told* people I was doing it. I was accountable for results!

In 2011, years of frustration finally ended. Motivation ceased to be an issue after I took an unscheduled trip to an amazing place in June. Then in November, I was laid off and time was abruptly no longer a problem either. Although these events were completely out of my control, they each occurred at precisely the right time. As the summer of 2011 melted into autumn, the alignment of those two events allowed me to gradually come to understand why thoughts about Destiny had nagged at me for so many years, and to understand why sharing those thoughts with you is so necessary.

Suddenly, writing *Undiscovered Horizons* took on a rather immediate personal urgency because I now had evidence that Personal Destiny is real. I was called to write this book because understanding that reality is critically important—to you, to your family and friends, to everyone who lives on earth today, and to those who will arrive in the future. You have a Personal Destiny. That means that you come to this life with a very specific role to play, for which no one else in the world has been prepared.

Destiny is not about what you'd like to be, or what you want to be. Rather, it's about why you're here and who you're here to be. *Undiscovered Horizons* tells the story of what I saw first-hand during an amazing visit to Heaven—that God-given Destiny is real, that you have a specific purpose for being here that was defined by God before you were born, that He prepared you in advance to fulfill that purpose, and that whether you fulfill it or not is up to you. This book is a personal roadmap to your own Undiscovered Horizon, and to what lies beyond it. Once you find and achieve your unique role—whatever it is—you'll live a life of reward and fulfillment that is beyond the farthest reaches of your imagination.

Just before sitting down to organize my notes and write the final version of this book, I discovered that there were 692 books on destiny-related topics for sale on Amazon.com. That's a lot of ink devoted to one topic and I wondered if I would have anything to say that hadn't already been said. As I looked through many of the books and their descriptions, I saw career guides, books on doing what you love, women's Bible study guides, books on Eternal Destiny, personal strategic planning workbooks and books on passion.

Many of those 692 books were based on the premise that Destiny is something that can be, or even should be, created or shaped or determined by the reader. Many were written in a "how-to" format, with step-by-step instructions. Every book I looked at was written by a capable author who wanted to share a well-thought-out message of value with people like you. Several are books I would recommend you read. Some of them I already own. Yet, in the midst of this sea of ink devoted to Destiny, I saw that the literary world had, in fact, left McComb with something to say on the subject . . . something that hadn't been said before.

Undiscovered Horizons—book #693—is not about discovering your passion; it's about discovering *why* you're passionate. This message is unique because it's about a specific kind of journey few others have taken, to be shown something that no one else has seen, in a way in which no one else has been taught. This story is unique because it's my story, the story of how I came to learn that earthbound Personal Destiny exists, apart from Eternal Destiny; the story of how I came to learn that you and I were each born with a unique purpose that was crafted for us long before the day we ever drew our first breath. It's the story of how I came to learn that there *is* a way for you to discover your own Personal Destiny, that there *is* a distinct path you can take to fulfill it, and that the path *is* waiting for you as you read these words. It's my story, but I've tried to tell it so you'll recognize it as *your* story. You'll discover *your* Personal Destiny while sharing the journey I took to find mine.

This is the first preface I have ever written. In fact, I looked up the word "preface" to see what is generally included in one. I learned that it discusses how the idea for the book was developed and how the book eventually came into being. I think I've covered the book idea and development here without being too long-winded, but I'd also like to include something beyond the standard definition. I'm concluding this preface with a direct appeal to those of you who have chosen to read this book.

As you prepare to read Chapter One, I ask each of you to make this commitment—to me, and to yourself:

- You will *read the entire book*, all the way to the end. The last eight words are critical to your future, but you won't know what they mean or how to act on them until you've read the entire book.
- You will *read the book with an open mind*. Regardless of your faith, this book has a message that is unique to you. Be slow to say, "I don't believe it" or "I don't agree," and quick to say, "I'll reserve judgment until I've read it all."
- As you read about what I experienced and learned and saw, you will *think about similar experiences and lessons in your own life*. This may be my story, but as you read, you need to see it as your story.
- You will *answer, on paper—for your future use—any questions I might ask you* to ponder in the book. You'll never reach the Horizon if you haven't planned for the trip.
- You will *share your feelings about the book with someone you love*. No one pilots a solo flight through Life. There is always someone special in the co-pilot's seat.
- You will *apply what you learn to your own life, and take action*. If you don't do this, then you've wasted your time and money on this book. Our lives are too short to waste a single minute and our resources are too precious to waste a single dollar.
- You will *email me* at <u>JimMcComb@UndiscoveredHorizons.com</u> *with your thoughts about the book* and its impact on you and your life. I want to do more than sell a book. I want to build a relationship with each reader and I want to know

how, if at all, this book has transformed lives. In other words, I want to know if I've fulfilled my own Destiny.

If you make—and fulfill—this commitment, I'm convinced that *Undiscovered Horizons* will become the most important book you'll ever read. Unless, of course, you've read the Bible.

Jim McComb
San Dimas, California
April 14, 2013

Acknowledgements

From the time that the notion of Personal Destiny first came to my mind, until the publisher delivered the first book to my doorstep, *Undiscovered Horizons* has been a labor of love. Hundreds of people have shared the journey with me and while space limitations make it impractical to mention everyone, I would like to thank a number of very special people who ensured that my personal Horizon would not go Undiscovered.

My most heartfelt thanks are reserved, of course, for my wife Sally. She is my best friend, my cheerleader, and God's choice to be my partner throughout the remainder of my days on this earth. She spent money she didn't really have to send me on a surprise two-week sojourn to a mountain cabin to write a substantial portion of the final manuscript, and has been there to encourage me through every all-nighter and every publisher's deadline.

I will always be grateful to my daughter, Laura McComb Wolhart; to my Mom & Dad, Jan and Jim McComb; to my brother Barry and sister Wendy, to my first wife, Cindy Frith; to my junior high school English teacher, Miss Josephine Mathews; to my mentor, Steve Haines; and to my good friends Janice Laureen and Gary McDonald for each having played a significant role in making me the person I am today.

Deep appreciation to Debby Englander for her kind assistance in editing the manuscript; to Rob and Diane Barilone of Preferred Choice Printing in Corona, California, for their prayer support during some of my darkest hours and for their work on the *Undiscovered Horizons Destiny Plan* workbook; to my friends Laura Brown, Kate Bernhardt, Griff Griffis and Torri Deming for reviewing parts of the manuscript and giving me honest—and valuable—opinions, and to Scott Hamilton for his guidance over the past couple of years.

Deep appreciation also to Steve Harrison and Geoffrey Berwind of Bradley Communications in Philadelphia for helping me understand how to better tell my story and how to more effectively share it with others; to Brian Edmondson for rescuing my boring website; to Sabrina Gibson for working her social media magic on my behalf; to Ann McIndoo, my book coach; to Bruce Carse, who helped me discover the power in storytelling; to Laura Atchison, a fellow author who helped me rediscover my passion; to fellow author Marcia Wieder, who taught me to dream again; to Rick Frishman for introducing me to so many amazing people through Author101 University; and to Thomas Bahler and Sally Anderson and Wendy Lipton-Dibner for inspiring me when no one else could.

There are several people I want to thank just because they will always be very special to me and several of them never stopped asking, "Is the book done?" They held my feet to the fire and I am grateful to God for making them a part of my life: Rose Kruggel, Pete Kucma, Tim Trotter, Isabel Gonzalez, Peggy McHugh, Sin Yi Lambertson, Pastor Ed Selvidge, Ken Pingel, Tony Shipley, Diane and Dave McCue, Steve Waffle, Steve Gebhardt, Melissa Miller, Rosalind Henderson, Diana Waters, Peggy Morris, Randy and Sara Bulow, Kathy Milner, Tara Gray, Deb Boelkes, Scott McCrary, Roger Reitzel, Art Douglas, Deborah Lamborghini, Alan Leeds, Dr. Stan Rosen, Gary Newcomer, Dr. David Crain, Bob Skubal, Rick Lapi, Mark Rydberg (RIP Mark), Jody Padfield, Jeff Freeman and Nancy Wolfson, Robert Zavala, Vicky Peth, Peg Loftis Hanyak, Zeke Baissa, Chuck Cadena (RIP Chuck), Stephanie Cameron,

John Gunderson, Lori Heredia, Rev. Murray and Sue Frick, Gary Trumpp, Evelyn Zeller, Rich Jett, Jim Kee, Vic DiMichina, Linda Kersey, Mickey Mixon, John Nigh, Cynder Niemela, Richard Pai, Dr. Joyce Reynolds-Sinclair, Toni Roldan, Peter Sharoff, Seena Sharp, Alex Urmersbach, Ellen Walsh, Molly Walpola and Ron Staake.

Of course, I can't forget my very special fellow authors and Quantum Leap buddies, Denise Krochta, Liz Cassidy, Shari McGuire, Greg Walsh, Laura Brown, Kate Bernhardt, Cydney O'Sullivan, Meryl Nieman, Lorraine Justice, Catherine D'Agostino, Dara Feldman, Diane Ross, Jill Caro, Ikumi Kayama, Bob Ragazzo, Winifred Bragg, and Teresa Wallace.

Finally, the most important acknowledgement of all: eternal gratitude to the Father, the Son and the Holy Spirit, without whom there would be no book, no Jim McComb, no Destiny, and no hope for the future of humankind.

1

Life: It's No Accident

*There is no such thing as chance;
and what seems to us to be merest accident
actually springs from the deepest source of destiny.*

Friedrich Schiller (1759-1805)
Poet, philosopher, historian, playwright

The alarm went off that morning at 3:30. It was the usual time, and an every-day ritual. I got up, showered, had breakfast while I watched the news, drove six miles to the park-and-ride and took my place in line to catch the 5:15 bus that would take me another twenty-three miles west on the 210 freeway to Pasadena. The bus was two minutes late, but I didn't think anything of it. It was raining, but I hardly noticed. The bus driver chose not to use the car pool lane that morning, but my nose was buried in my *USA Today* and nothing else mattered.

About halfway to Pasadena, I heard the other riders on the bus gasp and looked up just in time to see a horrific pileup in the car pool lane. Several cars had rear-ended each other as they braked and skidded on the slick roadway. People in Southern California always drive too fast in the car pool lane, even on dry pavement, and the road to Pasadena has its share of blind curves that trick fast-moving motorists until it's too late. I'm not sure what caused this particular wreck, but it was a doozy. One car was upside down. A couple of others were on fire, and yet another sat in the car pool lane facing the wrong way. A box truck was somehow involved as well.

As we drove by, I noticed that someone had been ejected from his vehicle and was lying in the roadway, being attended to by onlookers. The first responders were still en route. It was a tragic scene, and I can remember thinking at the time that this one split-second event had triggered a seemingly endless series of repercussions that would echo across families and workplaces for days, and perhaps weeks, to come.

For years, I had believed that Life was a series of random events and crazy coincidences, linked only by the indiscriminate choices we made from among the results of those coincidences. But now, as the accident faded from view, I wondered if Life wasn't actually a carefully orchestrated adventure instead, leading toward a specific destination that is pre-determined for each of us. What if just one of those cars had chosen a lane other than the car pool lane at that particular moment? What if just one of them had left home five minutes sooner, or had been driving five miles an hour slower, or had . . . ?

I pondered the same series of "what-ifs?" for our bus. The driver is never late, but he was that morning. He *always* uses the car pool lane, but for some reason he didn't that morning. Normally, we would have been traveling in the car pool lane, in about the same spot, at about the same time the accident occurred. But that day, we weren't where we normally would have been, at the time we would have been there. Had fate intervened on our behalf? Likewise, had it intervened to bring those involved in the crash together for some unknown purpose?

Life, truly, is no accident. The evidence is everywhere.

Accidental Romance?

Life shows us that it's no accident in many ways. As you know, the course of your life changes every day because of the decisions and the choices you make. Some decisions are as seemingly insignificant as the time you'll decide to leave the office tonight, the people with whom you chose to connect on social media this afternoon, or the news program you watched early this morning as you ate breakfast. Others are Life's really significant choices . . . career changes, moves to other states or cities, faith commitments, marriage, divorce, bankruptcy, entering the military, whether or not to have children.

Yet all decisions—whether insignificant or not—wind up being significant because they determine who you'll meet during the day, where you'll be at any given moment, what you'll be talking about or thinking about, and even why you'll choose to make other decisions in the way that you do. Often, you'll make the decisions that you do because you *know* that they're the right ones to make and that it's the right time to make them. You're *led* to make them, but you're not always sure why. That's when Life steps up and shows you that something that *seemed* so accidental actually had purpose.

For example, among the most significant decisions I ever made in my life were the choices of the two women I married. The first, Cindy, gave me eighteen years filled with great memories and tremendous personal growth. While partnered with her I became a parent, something that I'm sure will always rank as the most profound and rewarding experience of my life. Although Cindy and I divorced in 2000, she remains someone for whom I have only the highest respect and admiration. I definitely wouldn't trade the eighteen years I spent with her for anything.

Six months before I married Cindy, I didn't even know her. We met while working on the state senate campaign of a man named Cub Houck in Oregon in 1980. Cindy worked with Cub's wife, Kathy, in the coronary unit at Salem Hospital. I had been introduced to Cub through friends I knew by virtue of working for a politically active Executive Officer at the Salem Homebuilders Association and Board of Realtors. Although Cub didn't know me, for some reason he asked me to fill a management role in his campaign. Cindy was his volunteer coordinator. We met, all because of the workplaces we chose and the people whom we chose as friends.

If either of us had made even one insignificant choice differently along the way, we would never have met and married. We would not have the daughter we have today, and I would not be the person I am today. It was her expertise as a nurse that led her to insist that I leave work one morning in August 2006 and get to the hospital. I was bleeding internally and didn't know it. Inclined to stay at work because I had a busy day ahead, I would have died had I not heeded her concerned insistence. She was already my ex-wife at the time, and was three states away, but she saved my life on the phone that day . . . setting me on a course to write this book for you. Life is no accident.

I married my second wife, Sally, on the front porch of the Grand Hotel on Mackinac Island in Michigan on October 16, 2010. We were dressed in attire from 1912 (as was everyone else in the hotel that day), and no one in our wedding party—including the Best Man and the Matron of Honor—knew us 48 hours before the wedding. Nor did any of the 800 guests we paraded in front of that evening in the hotel parlor.

So, why even mention this bizarre wedding? Because it is exceeded in its "bizarr-ity" only by the incredible coincidences that led us to meet in the first place. First, though, let me say that I am incredibly fortunate to have married a second woman for whom I *also* have only the highest respect and admiration. As I write this, we have only been married for two years, but I already have amassed a lifetime's worth of memories. In that short time, I have grown and changed more profoundly—and for the better—than during any other era in my life. I truly look forward to spending the rest of my life with this amazing woman. She is truly my soul mate, and a gift from God.

I almost never met her. During the ten years between the end of my first marriage to Cindy and the beginning of my marriage to Sally, I was a committed bachelor. I told people that I had been single long enough to like it. But I also dated very actively and had a brush or two with the altar. I was a committed fan of one of the big online dating sites, although I took a break to try a competitor. I was on the competitor for six months in their early years and never met a single woman. The communication channels were obsessively controlled by them through email questions with multiple choice responses and the matches were selected by them as well. That process was the opposite of what I was used to on the other site, and I hated it.

I vowed I would never leave my favorite site again, and then, years later, for some inexplicable reason, I took a vacation from them and went back to the competitor. To this day, I couldn't tell you why. I was on the competitor site for a month and the first woman I dated thought she was God's gift to men and our date at Disneyland was a class-A disaster. I never went back on that site again, but my profile was still up because I had purchased a six-month membership. Forty-five days later while I was at a conference in Orlando, I got an email from Sally, who had seen my profile and wanted to meet. I wasn't sure, but we got into an instant message exchange, followed by a telephone conversation that lasted most of the night.

The conference was over and I flew back to Los Angeles in the morning. We met in the parking lot at Red Lobster that night and have been together ever since. The minute I laid eyes on her, I knew we were destined to be together. Yet if I had purchased a shorter membership, we never would have met. Two years later, it was her prompt action that got me to a hospital emergency room, saving my life and continuing me on the course to write this book for you. Yet again, Life was no accident.

Curve Balls

Whether you're married or not, you are now undoubtedly thinking about the decisions you've made over the years in your own life . . . where to work, where to live, who to befriend, and the myriad of decisions that simply come under the heading of "how to live." It's almost overwhelming when you think of where you might be today if you had made just one decision differently, like majoring in something different in college, or turning down that blind date, or moving to Vermont instead of New Mexico.

The fact is, Life is Not an Accident. We make decisions throughout our lives that are meant to be made, to lead us in the direction in which we're intended to go. The decisions I've made throughout my life lead me, eventually, to write this book and to share it with you. Decisions you've made throughout your life brought you to the point of buying and reading this book. The day I finished writing *Undiscovered Horizons*, and the day you'll finish reading it, are each days that will change us forever and set us both on a path to fulfill our life's purpose . . . to do the things that we were each born to do.

Now think for a moment about those times when Life has made decisions for you. How many times has the course of your existence been altered because you woke up late, or because an unknown person thrust their hand into yours at a party or a business gathering, or because your car broke down, or because a friend asked for a favor you weren't expecting to have to do, or because an unsolicited and unexpected job opportunity landed in your lap? You'll never know how many triumphs or tragedies you've missed because Life threw you a curve ball, but one thing *is* certain. When those curve balls came, you swung the bat a little differently and your life veered off of the path you had *planned* to take, toward the path that you were *destined* to take. As you traveled that new path, you inevitably encountered new triumphs and trials that you would not have experienced had the curve balls never come. Triumphs and trials that brought newfound opportunity to your life . . . opportunity that would otherwise have gone undiscovered.

Think, too, about how vast the world is, and how random events seem. Yet every day, people emerge out of the mass of humanity that inhabits that vast world. They cross your path and many have a transformational impact on your life, as Cindy and Sally have had on mine. And when you think about the circumstances that led you to meet those people, and allowed you to develop sustained relationships with them, you'll realize that one simple decision—made in the wake of a decision Life made for you—could have sent your paths off in opposite directions. You would never have met, and you would not be the person you are today.

The same is true of opportunities that come to you out of that same vast world, every single day. Often, they're opportunities you didn't even seek or create on your own, but they come to you anyway and like relationships, they, too, have a transformational impact on your life. And, as with relationships, when you think about the circumstances that brought those opportunities into your life, and allowed you to leverage them, you'll again realize that one simple decision—made in the wake of a decision Life made for you—could have caused an opportunity to have been lost forever.

The decisions you've made on your own, and the curve balls, people and opportunities that Life has brought to you over the years have shaped your life and are largely responsible for the person you are today. And so it goes from here. Right now there are people and opportunities waiting to fundamentally transform you and send your life in an entirely new direction someday.

Finding & Fulfilling Your Destiny: Step One

One of the major reasons that so many of us who inhabit the world don't know why we're here is that we've failed to recognize the signs of what is truly important in our lives. We haven't swung at the curve balls because we didn't see them coming. We haven't fully connected with the transformational people who've crossed our path because we didn't recognize them. We haven't leveraged the life-changing opportunities that came our way because we weren't able to identify them.

The first step in finding and fulfilling your own unique Personal Destiny is recognizing that things happen in your life for a reason, that significant people and opportunities are purposefully injected into your life. It is critical to understand the potential impact they can have on shaping your life and why that impact is important.

Heaven Revealed

Early in the summer of 2011, I took that first step toward finding and fulfilling my own Destiny when I experienced an amazing journey and discovered, along the way, the ultimate proof that Life is no accident. It all began on the day that changed my life forever. The day I died.

June 6, 2011. The day before my 57th birthday. It was just an ordinary day for June in Los Angeles. Sunny. A slight breeze. Upper 70's. No fatalities on the freeways. The Dodgers lost to the Phillies in Philadelphia and the Angels lost to the Tampa Bay Rays in Anaheim. Jerry Springer had another televised on-stage brawl, the World Newsstand was back in business in Laguna Beach six months after a mud flow had taken it out, and losses in the financial sector drove the stock market down. Actress Lynda Carter sang songs from her new CD at the Barnes & Noble store at The Grove, and some of the southbound lanes of the 405 freeway near the Getty Center began to shut down for road construction. *X-Men: First Class* was the top movie, and the television airwaves were dominated by NBA playoff games. The *Los Angeles Times* obituaries in the days ahead would ultimately report that forty seven people had died in the city and its environs on June 6, 2011.

I also died that day, about midday, on an operating table in a small hospital an hour's drive from downtown. It happened during emergency surgery for a gall bladder that had ruptured weeks before, without my knowledge. My abdomen was teeming with gangrene and poisons were swirling around inside me, yet because of an odd course of events that began two months earlier, I didn't know it.

In early April, I had landed in the emergency room with severe chest pain, and an endoscopy revealed that I had a raging case of acid reflux that was altering the character of my esophagus. Released from the hospital a few days later, I had a prescription and orders to change my diet, and began fighting the enemy I knew about, rather than the more immediate—and more dangerous—enemy of which I was not yet aware.

On June 5, I was back in the emergency room with unbearable chest pain and an inability to breathe. Back in April I had been taken to a hospital that had a coronary unit since I had been having all of the symptoms of a heart attack. But this time, with the heart having already been eliminated as the source of my chest pain, I was delivered to a hospital that was closer to home and they did a scan that revealed that my gall bladder was missing in action. A technician had performed the same scan—with the same result—on me at the first hospital two months earlier. He called the results inconclusive and the hospital moved on to the endoscopy. Now, in a different hospital with a different technician, I thankfully got a different response to the scan results. My doctor received an immediate phone call.

Before long, I was wheeled into the operating room and prepared for surgery. This definitely had all the earmarks of an emergency surgery. The orderlies who had shoved my bed down the hall with lightning speed had very little to say to me, even though I was my usual chatty self. In the OR, the staff was engaged in an urgent hustle and there were looks of grim determination on most of the faces. Yet one of the nurses was talkative, and as the anesthetic was being administered, we were bantering about—of all things—football. I was talking about my beloved Denver Broncos, and she was telling me that I would be out soon. At least that's what I think was said because I was quickly drifting off to sleep, confused about my illness and about where my life was headed.

That all changed The Day I Went To Heaven.

Suddenly I awoke with a jolt, with the kind of power that occurs when you burst through the surface of a swimming pool after propelling yourself off the bottom because you've run out of air. For a split second after breaking the surface, you're a bit disoriented while you gulp for air and clear the hair and water out of your eyes. During my first moments after awakening, I was similarly disoriented. Rubbing my eyes, I felt an immediate rush of sheer terror flow through my body.

My eyes scanned a room that was completely foreign to me, and any thoughts I had of my trip to the hospital, my stay in the emergency room, or the preparations that were made before I lost consciousness in the OR had been erased from my memory banks. I last remembered having gone to bed after returning home from a Yankees-Angels game in Anaheim with my wife and another couple. In bed, in my own bedroom, I drifted off to sleep after a full evening of dinner, baseball and friends. Now, I was suddenly awakening to find myself standing in someone else's home.

I was in a room as real as the room I'm sitting in right now, as I write this passage. The floor was solid, yet soft and spongy like a foam mat. There were four stone walls that glittered, a large oaken door that was closed, and windows without glass—although I couldn't see through the openings for some reason. Furnishings were sparse. A massive wooden table and two chairs. As I got my bearings, I realized that this was unlike any room in which I had ever stood before.

Heaven didn't immediately come to mind as I gazed around the room. Although I've been a Christian all of my life, I had always pictured Heaven as a spiritual place without any particular shape or substance . . . a place where souls gathered to live in eternity with the Creator. Yet this room was real. It was physical, tangible and specific. Heaven? I wasn't sure. I couldn't remember dying, and hadn't been led through a tunnel or wandered around in any mist. My deceased parents, grandparents, and friends were not here to greet me. Heaven?

This particular room was bathed in an incredibly bright, white light that seemed to have no real, discernible source. It emanated from everywhere, yet came from nowhere, and had a strange golden tone to it. The room didn't appear to have a ceiling, or at least one that I could see, but I knew that this light wasn't from an overhead chandelier or from the sun. The light seemed to become a part of me, or perhaps I became a part of it. As the radiance washed over me, the terror drained out of my body and I felt an incredible sense of joy and peace and trust and unconditional love so tangible that it felt like a tiny newborn baby in the palm of my hand.

As the luminosity permeated my body I knew that, although I had never been here before, I was home. Music wafted into the room from somewhere. It had power and intensity, yet was soft and melodious and unlike any music I had ever heard before. As I strained to determine which instruments were responsible for this mysterious symphony, I realized that there were no musicians and no instruments. Rather, the music was a blend of human voices so perfect that it transcended the greatest effort of any earthbound choir that I had ever heard, or imagined. It was coming from nowhere in particular, yet it was coming from everywhere. The music reached a crescendo, blending perfectly with the light, and then, in the blink of an eye, that huge oaken door swung open and He was in the room with me.

It was as if the light and the music had morphed into a human form, although they were both still omnipresent when I first laid eyes on Him. He strode into the room, with a bit of a gliding motion to His step, and came to a stop about two feet from me, looking at me . . . and into me . . . with the most beautiful eyes I had ever seen. I've always believed that eyes are the most striking human characteristic, and I've seen thousands of pairs of them during my fifty-eight year lifetime. Yet none were as stunning as the eyes that were meeting mine at this moment.

He and I were about the same height, a couple of inches above six feet. His tousled brown hair, closely-cropped brown beard and chiseled features reminded me of the rugged good looks of a leading man in the movies, with a sort of rock star edge. The white robe and golden sash that He wore stood out in stark contrast to His olive skin and He was bathed in glowing light from head to toe that managed to outshine even the dazzling rays that naturally engulfed the room.

I was drawn to Him like metal is attracted to a magnet. His face was childlike and innocent, yet bore the lines of an experienced elder statesman. Kindness and love and patience and forgiveness all resided in that face. It was an inviting face, an accepting face, a face that seemed to incorporate all of humanity into a single, subtle smile . . . into a tiny twinkle in the corner of His eye . . . into the gentle nod of His head.

He didn't communicate in the way that you and I would talk with each other. I just "knew" what He was saying, so He didn't *have to speak. His wishes and thoughts "came" to me, just as God has been speaking to me for years. I didn't hear a voice, per se; I just "knew" what I was supposed to hear, and to do. He has always conversed with me through intuition and conscience, rather than through a bass voice booming from the heavens. I'm sure that He communicates with you in the same way.*

As I said, I was captivated by Him. Compelled to become a part of Him. I wanted to reach out and touch Him but I was awestruck, intimidated and fearful, although perfectly at peace at the same time. Suddenly, just as I felt an overwhelming desire to lift the fingers of my left hand to His face, I also sensed a sort of divine permission to touch Him. I did. I reached out and grazed the side of His face with my fingertips. It was unlike anything I had ever felt before. Softer than the softest blanket, yet as electrifying as soaring over the Grand Canyon on a hang glider. My hand seemed to melt into His face, and a rush of love and peace and utter joy burst through my arm and into my body like electric current recharging a battery. At once, I felt invigorated and re-energized. Self-doubt and fear drained out of me at that moment and I felt ready for whatever lay ahead in Life.

He never formally introduced Himself. He didn't have to. His countenance. His touch. His authority. I recognized them all. I was in the presence of Jesus Christ Himself, and I had awakened in Heaven. It was real. It was now. It was no dream, no hallucination, and no accident. It was Life. It had a Purpose.

Reflecting back on this "arrival," I know that it was no garden-variety near-death experience. There was no mist, no darkness, no tunnel, and no friendly faces of loved ones to tell me it "wasn't my time" and that I must "return" to the life I was living. This was no typical brush with Eternal Life. Clearly, I had been brought here for a very specific purpose. While no one told me that it was "not yet my time," I knew that my stay would be temporary. I sensed that I had been brought here specifically to be taught something that I would be expected to impart to others later, including you.

Secrets Shared

This book is about what I discovered in Heaven, about knowledge revealed to me specifically for the purpose of sharing it—and the expectations and responsibilities that come with it—with you. You are among the very first to hear my story, although, as you will see soon enough, it is actually your story.

The Day I Went To Heaven occurred in June 2011, yet I didn't share details of it with anyone until I told my wife in March 2012. Even then, I revealed little. Much of what she knows of my experience she learned a year later when I gave her the finished manuscript to read. In spite of the Destiny written for me by God, and His directive to fulfill that Destiny, I was reluctant to share what had happened to me. I knew there would be skeptics. Those who would say it was a lie, or a dream, or a hallucination caused by all of those things that happen to the brain when a person dies. Or perhaps they would just think I was crazy because, after all, *no one really goes to Heaven and comes back to talk about it* because, of course, we *all* know there is no such place.

I guess I can't prove that I'm not crazy, although those who know me would tell you that I seem normal enough (at least I *hope* they would tell you that). The Day I Went To Heaven, I was a senior vice president at a Fortune 100 company, a past national president of a professional association, and had been elected—and re-elected—to public office. I was leading a life that seemed credible and normal, although some would certainly question my sanity in running for public office.

My story can't be a lie, because the stakes are too high for someone like me who professes to be a Christian. Someday, when I leave this earth permanently, I will have to explain this to God Himself if it is a lie. No Christian would relish that conversation. Besides, since all of us will pass from this life eventually, we will someday *all* learn the truth about every lie ever told. I certainly wouldn't want to face you—and everyone else who would ever read or hear about this book—every day for eternity if what I said here wasn't the truth as I experienced it.

In the weeks following The Day I Went To Heaven, I read everything I could find about what happens to the brain when a person dies. Many scientists and researchers feel that those who claim to have seen Heaven are hallucinating, but I know that wasn't my experience. Someone who sees an oasis in the middle of the Sahara Desert is hallucinating because, try as they might, they can never reach that oasis. They can't touch it, they can't taste the water, and they can't interact with it in any way because it isn't there. My senses—all five of them—were fully engaged while I was in Heaven. I was able to interact with it because it *was* there. My experience was *not* a hallucination.

I also know that it wasn't a dream. I remember vivid details as though they happened to me last Tuesday, just as I clearly remember what I *did* do last Tuesday . . . watching the lizard in the driveway scurry out of the way when I put the trash cans out, once again forgetting which way to turn on Alton Parkway in order to get to Taco Bell headquarters in Irvine for a meeting, tipping the Korean woman who handles my dry cleaning. I usually don't remember my dreams at all, and when I do, they are soon forgotten in the hustle and bustle of Life. But I will *never* forget this.

Dreams—particularly mine—also rarely seem to make any sense. I'm usually in places that don't make sense, doing things that don't make sense, with an assortment of people who have no sensible connection to each other. My dreams always look like motion pictures . . . something I'm watching that streamed in from Netflix, rather than the three dimensional world in which I move about every day. And my dreams never seem to have a purpose or a logical outcome. My visit to Heaven had everything that my dreams never do . . . purpose, logic, dimension, and substance.

Most important of all, in my dreams I always seem to be an observer—even when I'm actually *in* the dream. In this case, I was an active participant and was in full command of all five of my senses. I heard the Heavenly chorus just as clearly as I heard my wife speak to me just a moment ago. I felt the face of Christ with the same intensity with which I now feel the keys of my laptop as I write this passage. I smelled the sweetness of Heaven just as distinctly as I now smell the aroma coming from our rose bushes as I sit on my patio at work on this book. I tasted the dryness in my mouth when I first gazed in awe upon the face of Christ just as surely as I now taste the moisture in my mouth from the bottled water that sits on the table in front of me. And I saw a river of color flowing in Heaven just as clearly as I now see fluffy white clouds drifting through the beautiful blue sky overhead.

It wasn't a dream. It wasn't electrical impulses firing in my brain. I wasn't hallucinating. Heaven is real . . . as real and as substantive as my home in San Dimas, California. And someday you will have a chance to experience the reality of Heaven for yourself. Just as everything in life occurs for a reason, The Day I Went To Heaven was no accident. It had a Purpose.

What If?

As I lay in the hospital the next day, June 7, 2011 (my 57th birthday), drifting in and out of consciousness, my mind inevitably centered on all of the "What if?" questions that had been prompted by the unlikely events of the previous couple of months . . . what if the results of the second gall bladder scan had been ignored, as those of the first were? What if I had become critically ill on the Caribbean cruise my wife and I took just a week before I was rushed to the hospital for the emergency surgery? What if we had waited just a little while longer before going to the hospital on June 5? Oh, what if . . . ?

Actually, the "Why didn't I?" questions soon outweighed "What if?" If my gall bladder had, indeed, ruptured in early April, why didn't I become seriously ill much sooner than June 5? If I could have died—permanently—before the surgery, then why didn't I become gravely ill on the cross country flight from Fort Lauderdale to Houston to Los Angeles that I had taken just a week earlier? Why didn't I press the technician for concrete test results at the first hospital in April? Oh, why didn't I . . . ?

The fact that none of these "What if?" or "Why didn't I?" questions ever came to pass seemed to me to be more than simply a peculiar series of coincidences. It was as if the Red Sea had parted at each precise moment when such a parting was needed. Problems stepped aside for me. Roadblocks disappeared. Given the experiences I had the day of my operation, I now knew why I caught so many breaks during the previous several weeks.

Life hadn't been an accident; I was meant to survive that day. I was destined to do something I hadn't yet done . . . destined to be someone I hadn't yet become.

2

Undiscovered Horizons

*The two most important days in anyone's life
are the day they're born, and
the day they discover why.*

William Barclay (1907-1978)
Theologian, author

For the first thirty five years of my life, I wanted to be President of the United States. I imagined it, contemplated it and obsessed over it. In ninth grade, I even planned it. For an assignment in typing class, I wrote a multi-page report that chronicled my ascendency to the White House and even included a timeline with dates. My fantasy included moving to Vermont, becoming mayor of Burlington, serving in the U. S. Senate and running for president in 1996. Had that scenario played out, I would have served what ultimately became Bill Clinton's second term and George W. Bush's first term. The September 11 terrorist attacks would have happened on my watch, providing me the opportunity to demonstrate the leadership that would have made me one of America's greatest presidents . . . or one of the most colossal presidential failures.

Now, forty-three years after I wrote that report, you and I both know that the picture it painted never reached canvas. I've never lived in Vermont, let alone ever set foot in Burlington. Serving on a school board in Oregon is the closest I've ever come to being mayor of any city, and sitting in the gallery as a tourist is the closest I've ever come to a seat in the U. S. Senate. Although I have met Bill Clinton, Bob Dole, Al Gore and George W. Bush, I didn't run against any of them for president in either 1996 or 2000. I never reached the White House because it was a dream, not a Destiny. It wasn't the "something" I was destined to do that I hadn't yet done. Being the president wasn't the "someone" I was destined to be but hadn't yet become.

Although I've always been a dreamer and a planner, for most of my life I never thought much about Destiny. I didn't know if I had one, and I didn't really care. Like you, and most everyone else who has ever walked the planet, I grew into adulthood with no clue why I was born or what I was supposed to do with my life. I never envisioned the "someone" I was meant to be, or the "something" I was meant to do. For me (and as I'm sure it also is for you), the meaning of Life, my true purpose, the reason I exist—whatever it is—has always remained a carefully guarded secret tucked away somewhere way out there on the Horizon . . . that place I could always see plainly, but could never quite seem to reach.

I didn't even really know what Destiny was until I began thinking about it for no apparent reason eight years ago. I started to write this book, but wandered aimlessly for the first six of those years because I didn't know where the thoughts were coming from or why in the world I was writing a book. I had no sense of purpose, no feeling of Destiny, no belief that I was headed in any logical direction where the book was concerned.

That all changed The Day I Went To Heaven.

Through His Eyes

So there I was, two feet from Christ, captivated by His eyes. Those mesmerizing eyes. Eyes that pierced the very heart of my soul with a gentleness that I had never known before, gentleness that was the perfect blend of judgment and compassion. Just as my hand had melted into His cheek when my fingertips grazed Him, my entire body now seemed to lose its shape and form as it was drawn into Him. Abruptly, it was as if my eyes became His. I was seeing my life, as I had lived it so far, through His eyes like they were some sort of viewer. Fifty-eight years' worth of recorded history. Many moments were pleasant reminiscences that came fondly to my mind's eye, while others were experiences that had departed from my memory banks long ago with an encouraging shove. Distasteful memories, I had chosen to let them simply drift into obscurity.

The most pleasant parts of my life—those that genuinely made me feel warm inside when I saw them replay—were always about helping others. Donating money I didn't always have to the Rescue Mission and the Salvation Army. Shoveling snow as a young boy in Illinois for an elderly neighbor, without ever asking for payment. Giving countless hours to charities like the March of Dimes and the Red Cross and the United Way. Coaching and teaching and counseling literally thousands of people, in formal classes, and in one-on-one sessions—often at no charge—to help them make decisions that led to more fulfilling, successful lives. What truly astonished me is that I saw instances of "counseling" others that went all the way back to my days as a first grader at R. K. Welsh Elementary School. The significance of that was yet to come.

My pride in serving others was short-lived though. While I enjoyed seeing my triumphs and joys, they weren't the only life clips on this highlight reel. Through His eyes, I also saw a lifetime of things I have tried to forget. Every mistake was there for me to relive. So was every wrong turn, every missed opportunity, and every poor choice. It seems that my life wasn't (and isn't) always about serving others, or following the rules, or living the Commandments. In vivid, full-color detail I re-lived every instance when I hurt others, and myself, by making the wrong choice, saying the wrong words, or doing the wrong thing. If I seemed to be an expert at anything in my life, it was at saying and doing the wrong thing.

As I watched my life unfold, I suddenly realized that I had not only borrowed His eyes but that I had literally become a part of Him. I could feel His overwhelming joy ripple through my body whenever I made decisions that were consistent with my life's purpose, and I shuddered with His feelings of profound sadness and disappointment whenever I headed down the wrong path and turned away from Him.

Just as I saw things appear before His eyes that I had just said and done a day or two ago, a huge tidal wave unexpectedly surged over what had been my life and washed it all away. Suddenly, there I was, at about the age of four or five, sitting on a beach in what I believe was Door County, Wisconsin. We used to vacation there when I was young. I was drenched from head to toe, and was crying. Beside me were the flattened remains of what had been a sand castle. An incoming wave had clobbered me, overrun the moat I had made and wiped out my work of art.

A large man then came over and knelt beside me to offer consolation; I recognized him as my father. He comforted me and pointed out that the wave had actually given me an opportunity to build an even bigger and better castle on higher ground. Soon I was laughing and smiling as my dad helped me create a new masterpiece in the sand. Through His eyes, I began to see the castle as a metaphor for my life. God washed away all of the poor choices and bad decisions I had made, and all of the hurtful things I had said and done. He was now kneeling beside me in the sand, offering an opportunity to seek forgiveness for the sins and mistakes of my past . . . an opportunity to go back to that day at the beach so long ago, to begin again and to replace the life I had lived with the life I was destined to live.

In the Presence of God

At this point, I was a bit confused. What, exactly, is the "life I was destined to live?" Destiny was a word I'd seen in poetry and heard in the movies, but I was unsure what it really meant and how it was relevant to my life. Christ, sensitive to my confusion and curiosity, took me back to a time years earlier than that day at the beach.

Through His eyes, I saw a drab hospital room. A young woman barely out of her teens was in the bed, and in spite of her girlish features, I recognized her as my mother. In her arms, she cradled a baby, and judging from her age I knew that baby was me. On a plain metal chair next to the bed sat my father, just a boy of twenty-two, with an excited twinkle in his eye.

Although I didn't know for sure, I imagined that my parents were envisioning a life of great things for me, as most parents—including yours—probably do when their babies are born. At that moment, just after birth, Life is a clean slate for a baby . . . a level playing field. The various heartbreaks and joys that accompany growing up, going to school, having a career and rearing a family of your own are still just distant future memories when you're a baby. Or are they?

As I pondered that question, wondering how it had come to mind in the first place, I suddenly became aware that I was no longer looking through the eyes of Christ; for the moment, I was no longer one with Him. The door through which He had initially entered the room was now open and Christ beckoned me to follow Him through it. Powerful rays of brilliant white light overwhelmed the doorway and spilled through it like an avalanche of unrestrained snow. Christ disappeared into it and I felt compelled to follow. I was in another room, but was it really a room? It was enormous, so massive that I could not see any of the walls or the ceiling. I could see the floor—or what I thought was the floor—and it frightened me at first. It looked like a glassy, golden pond and I was afraid to walk on it. My fear subsided when I looked down and saw my face reflected in it, alongside that of Christ.

The room was filled with the same dazzling light as the room in which I had first awakened, except that the radiance in this room blazed with intensity and warmth unlike anything I had ever felt or experienced before. As the light wrapped me in a comforting *blanket of unconditional love, I was overcome by awe and reverence and worship.*

Three-dimensional color streamed into the room from every direction, like a gentle tsunami, and swirled in a tornado-like cloud in the center of the room as it intertwined with the radiant light. Every color of the rainbow was there, as were many colors I was seeing for the first time. I felt a rush of wind on my face as the cloud whirled in front of me. The same beautiful music I had heard in the first room was present here as well—a chorus of voices perfectly knitted together as if finely-tuned instruments in a supernatural symphony—though it was louder now and seemed to float into the room from above. The music was a perfect complement to the thunder that reverberated within the cloud as it encircled something that I could not yet see.

I don't remember how the room was decorated or furnished because my immediate attention was drawn to the spiraling cloud of three-dimensional color and dazzling white light, shrouding what appeared to be a throne of enormous proportions. It stretched upward and was so large that it was beyond my field of vision. Near the point where the throne met the floor I squinted through the intense white light and noticed what looked to me to be the outline of a portion of an enormous foot. An angelic presence ringed the cloud, although I could not see the angels themselves.

All at once the feelings of awe and reverence and worship and love that I was experiencing ramped up to an even higher level and I was overcome with emotion more intense than anything I have ever felt during my lifetime. I realized, as I looked into the whirling rainbow as it collided with the dazzling golden white light, that I was in the presence of the Glory of God. I was in complete and total awe and fell down in worship. My emotions were raw, a mixture of wonder, fear and sheer exhilaration. Even though I have believed in the existence of God ever since I was old enough to know who He was, I honestly never thought that I would ever be in His presence or experience His Glory, at least until I died.

And then, suddenly, it came to me. Since awakening in Heaven, I hadn't once thought about death. Now, for the first time, I contemplated the possibility that I had died. It seemed strange to me that I couldn't remember how, when, or where I died. Going to bed after returning home from the Angels-Yankees game was all I could remember.

I soon learned that I had not died, at least not in the permanent sense of the word. God had brought me here to reveal my Personal Destiny through a review of my life. Apparently, He had been trying to get my attention for years and I had always managed to be pre-occupied with the more mundane things of Life. All at once, those nagging thoughts I'd had about Destiny for the past six years began to make sense. I wasn't here to see Him or to hear His voice, but I <u>was</u> here to be shown the earthbound purpose for which He had breathed life into me, and to learn to show others how to discover their own unique divine mission.

He communicated with me the way He always has since I was a child. There was no booming voice, no holographic image projected in front of me, no "man behind the curtain" controlling it all. He spoke to me telepathically, in a still small voice that only I could hear. I wondered why I was so important to Him . . . why I would be brought to Heaven when there are so many more important people on earth who must certainly have missions more vital than anything I would be asked to do. He was quick to answer.

Christ had shown me my own birth, and had brought me to the very foot of the Throne of God because it was important for me to understand that I already had a God-given earthbound Personal Destiny on the very day I was born. You did as well.

God's Sadness

Before our spirit ever has a body, God gives it an Eternal Destiny: to live with Him as a part of His family for eternity. To realize that Destiny, we must believe in God as the Creator, that the Bible is His Holy Word, that Jesus Christ is the Son of God and the only way to eternal salvation, and that we are saved from our sins by grace, through faith. We must recognize our inherently sinful nature, repent of our sins, seek forgiveness through Christ, and live a Christ-like life while on earth.

Knelt in awe in that glorious room, a place where no one is sad or sick, I became painfully aware that some things do truly sicken God. Obviously, Sin is at the head of that list, as is the lack of desire by so many people to do anything about atoning for their sins. Many of us are already aware of God's position on Sin, but most people don't know that there is something else that brings God profound sadness as well.

As I fell down in worship in that magnificent room I also learned that, before we're born, God prepares each of us for a very specific earthbound Destiny that is so unique no one else is given the capacity to fulfill it. Not another living soul. Achieving that Destiny is a key part of living a Christ-like life, and is therefore vital to the ultimate fulfillment of our Eternal Destiny. God's profound sadness lies in the fact that so many of us never discover our earthbound Destiny, let alone pursue it. Later, I would learn that His sorrow was the reason I was in Heaven that day.

Sadly, most of us never connect with the word "destiny" because we don't understand the concept, or even think that it could be real. For some of you it's just a joke, something found only in romance novels or movie scripts. While writing this book, I imagined how I will be ridiculed and challenged by those of you who don't believe in God-given Destiny. I might even become fodder for the likes of late-night comics like Bill Maher or David Letterman.

Many of you do believe in Destiny, but simply view it as unattainable, or intimidating, or scary. Perhaps you envision larger-than-life images of larger-than-life people doing larger-than-life things that impact vast numbers of people worldwide for decades into the future. Most of you don't see yourselves as important enough to ever have that kind of impact.

Others of you who believe in Destiny spend a lifetime searching for it and eventually give up in frustration because the answers don't come easy enough. You presume that anything that difficult to figure out can't possibly be real. So, in the end, you conclude that Destiny doesn't exist and that Life has no deeper meaning beyond being born, doing the best you can at playing the game, and leveraging whatever advantages you've been given. Some of you never bother to look for it in the first place because you have a successful career, a loving family and friends, faith in God and lots of money. Who could want more?

I learned three very important things in Heaven . . . that Destiny is real, that each of you is born with a unique earthbound Personal Destiny to fulfill, and that each of you is equipped—at birth—to achieve something extraordinary during your lifetime . . . something that only you have been equipped to achieve that will have a lasting impact on humankind, reverberating across the decades of time long after you're gone. Your challenge is to seek that Destiny, discover it, and fulfill it. By reading to this point, you have already begun the search. In the pages that follow, through sharing more of what I learned The Day I Went To Heaven, you'll identify your unique life mission and learn how to fulfill it.

Destiny Defined

Most dictionaries define destiny as—among other things—a pre-determined course of events. Fate. Something set in motion in advance, leading to a specific result. Based on everything I learned and saw in Heaven, if God were to write a definition I believe He would say that it is "Life, as it was meant to be lived." In real life though, Destiny isn't always as precise as it is in the dictionary and the result isn't always as desirable as it is in God's Plan, simply because of a thing called Free Will. We often make decisions and choices in Life that can alter our course and undermine our Destiny. The fact is, most of us do that and miss out on the fulfillment that God intended when he equipped us for Life.

But when we don't undermine our Destiny with poor choices and bad decisions, what does it look like? As I worshipped at the foot of His Throne, this is the picture God painted:

Destiny is a calling that is woven into the fabric of your very existence, involving every aspect of your life, including faith, family, career, finances, health, friendships, service to others, romance, leisure and rest, lifelong learning and the very essence of your character. It's about being and doing; it's a role you fill that is much larger than any job or career or avocation.

Your Destiny is your mission. The basic, fundamental purpose of your life, it's about serving others: what you do, who you do it for and the lasting value or benefit of what you do. Destiny shapes your values and drives your vision of the future. It's about spiritual fulfillment, and isn't about money or fame or power or ego or pride or limits or fear.

Destiny always achieves extraordinary ends when it is fulfilled, though often in seemingly small ways. For example, a teacher's Destiny might be to touch just a single life in an entire lifetime of teaching. Yet, that single life might be the person who finds the ultimate cure for cancer, or the person who negotiates lasting peace in the Middle East, or the person who goes into teaching because of the example set by their teacher and, in turn, touches and inspires one very significant life.

Destiny is about more than doing what you love, or what you have passion for. It's about what you've been called to do, prepared in advance to do, and given the tools and skills and opportunities to do. Those who are doing what they've been called to do ARE doing something they love and are passionate about. Unfortunately though, it doesn't work both ways. Many of those doing what they love or what they're passionate about aren't doing what they have been called to do.

Fulfilling your Destiny will make you rich . . . perhaps financially, but definitely spiritually, morally and emotionally.

Your Destiny, quite simply, is the very essence of who you are and who you will become.

Destiny is Real

Suddenly, I noticed that Christ was focused on me. I looked deep into His eyes and felt myself once again become a part of Him. Soon I was gazing through those eyes at a succession of events featuring young children. Some had obviously been young a long time ago, while others were no doubt children right now.

I saw boys and girls from all over the world, none older than eight or nine and some as young as just four. They were engaged in a variety of pursuits normally reserved for adults as much as ten times their age. They were taking (and teaching) college classes, conducting medical research and studying to be doctors, composing symphonies, perfecting engineering skills, writing novels and poetry, and solving complex problems. One began to paint at the age of nine months and is an internationally renowned artist—right now—at the tender age of five.

I was surprised to see so many examples of exceptional ability at such young ages. Through Christ, I learned that we all have a core talent, just like each of the children I saw. We're all prodigies at something, yet most of us have intrinsic talents that don't manifest themselves until later in life, such as leading, organizing, counseling, teaching, planning and critical thinking. Even those talents, though, are already present when we're born.

In what seemed like an instant, I was shown that all of us have a role in Life, created for us before we ever arrive here. We each have an intrinsic talent that rolls out of the womb with us, but most of us never recognize it—or develop it—until it's too late, if ever. That intrinsic talent is the cornerstone of your earthbound Personal Destiny.

Think about the times in your life—and I'll bet there have been several—when a relative or a co-worker or a friend or, in a rare instance, a complete stranger has said something like this to you: "Rebecca, you're a natural leader" or "Juan, you're an inspirational speaker" or "Tamika, you're a gifted writer," or a talented entertainer, teacher or counselor. Chances are that many people have made similar observations about you during your lifetime, and they have probably all mentioned the exact same talent or attribute. When you stop to think about what they've said, you realize that you *are* as talented as they say. You have an ability that never took any study or practice, clearly placing you at a level far ahead of those who *do* study and practice.

After hearing so many people—over so many years—comment on your gift, you no doubt say to yourself, "You know, I *am* good at that, and you know something else? I'm not really sure *why*

I'm good at it. I never took a class to learn how to do it. I never asked anyone to show me how to do it. And I don't even have to concentrate very hard to be good at it. I just *am*. I guess I was just born to be good at it." *That* is Destiny. Each of you has a God-given talent inherent in your character, wired into your DNA, woven into the very fabric of who you are. And that God-given talent has a purpose.

Most of the greatest leaders never went to leadership school. Many of the most inspirational speakers were never members of Toastmasters, and most of the greatest thinkers and scholars never hired a coach to show them how to think or learn. For virtually all of you, the one thing you're best at—that thing others always notice you're best at—is almost always something that no one ever taught you or showed you how to do. While you might have sought some coaching or coursework in order to get *better*, you nevertheless were born with that talent. Surely, that inherent gift is there to be used for a specific pre-determined purpose in Life.

Surrounding that intrinsic, core talent is a suite of skills, abilities, talents and interests, most of which are also inherent in you at birth and develop as you grow. Coming into this world endowed with a specific, one-of-a-kind treasure trove of assets that no one else has in that exact combination can only mean one thing: those tools are meant to be used to build something unique, to leave a legacy no one else can leave, to be used in the combination that only you were given . . . to fulfill a specific purpose that is uniquely yours.

Intrinsic talents and unique skill sets provide compelling evidence for the existence of Destiny. Evidence even more compelling was yet to come.

The Office

Anticipating what some of the readers of this book might wonder, I prepared to ask Christ if there really is a specific role for everyone. After all, the world is a big place. There are billions of people on this planet. Are there enough Destinies to go around? Many of those people are hungry, or in war zones, or are under the thumb of oppressive regimes. They couldn't possibly have an earthbound Destiny, or care about it even if they did. Is there really a role for everyone?

I wheeled around to confront Christ with these questions and felt myself drift into Him again. Once more, I was gazing through His eyes, a lucky break since He had just prevented me from doing something I would have eternally regretted: challenging Him (and in Heaven, no less!). This time, I saw my work team in the mortgage finance group at Bank of America in Pasadena, California. Fourteen people were at their desks working. Actually, only thirteen desks were occupied. There was an empty seat. Mine. Part of the team was missing.

In that office I fulfilled a specific role every day of the work week, something that is true in factories, offices, farm fields, classrooms, laboratories and home offices around the world every day. You fulfill a specific role as well. What if you called in sick tomorrow, or were on vacation, or abruptly quit or got fired? What if you weren't there, in your workplace, to fulfill your responsibilities? You are missing, just as I was on The Day I Went To Heaven. Suddenly, there is a hole in the workflow. Everyone on the team is there for a reason, to play a specific role. But you're not there.

The boss has several choices. He or she can ask your colleagues to take a portion of your work, or call in a temporary worker to do it, or leave it undone until you return. None of those choices gets the work done in exactly the same manner in which you would have done it. Your employer hired you because of the unique set of talents, skills and abilities you brought to the job. No one else can duplicate that, particularly people who are trying to do your work in addition to theirs. Even if they try, they can't do it quite as efficiently, or as effectively, or as thoroughly as you would have.

The fact that your job doesn't get done, or is done less effectively, has ripple effects on the people around you, on your customers and on the entire organization. The customer isn't served as well as you would have served them. Your co-workers are less effective than they would have been without shouldering your workload too. The owners might make a little less money than you would have earned for them.

Therefore, Life isn't as it should be—in Pasadena or in your workplace—because you and I are not there to meet our responsibilities and fulfill our roles.

Just as I was wondering how my office, and my absence, could justify the existence of Destiny, my office melted into a view of the world as one vast office. Through His eyes, I immediately noticed that most of the chairs were empty. Puzzled for a moment, I thought that most of the world certainly could not have called in sick today. I felt Him smile for a moment, but His countenance quickly shifted to concern as He explained that the empty chairs represented those who were not fulfilling their earthbound Personal Destiny. I didn't know which chair out in the vast expanse of the world was mine, but I was certain it was empty at this moment.

Sin is the overarching reason for the world's problems, and I understood that long before I ever arrived in Heaven. But I was now learning something that I didn't know. The world is meant to run just like a finely-tuned workplace: each of us, specially prepared for a specific Personal Destiny, pursues and fulfills that Destiny every day. When we do that, it's tantamount to showing up for work at our office every day. Things run smoothly.

Failing to discover, understand, and fulfill our Destiny is the equivalent of calling in sick. Your chair in that vast world office is empty, and the course of our collective existence is altered because the right person is not doing the right thing in the right place at the right time. No one qualified and prepared for your particular role is there to fill in for you.

So Personal Destiny is not only critical to the ultimate fulfillment of our individual lives, it is critical to the ultimate fulfillment of our collective existence on earth as well. That was a bombshell for me. I had no idea how vital my solitary, ordinary life (and yours as well) is to the lives of others and to the future of humankind. We are all, truly, instruments of God while we walk this earth.

It is essential to the future of the world that as many of us as possible discover why we're here and take steps to fulfill our Personal

Destinies. Most of us live our entire life without ever knowing what we were born to do, and so—obviously—we never do it. We're not in the right place, at the right time, positioned to do the right thing. Millions of us throughout history have missed our calling, causing millions of others to miss the benefits that would have accrued to society if only we had believed in Personal Destiny, known how to discover it, and committed to fulfill it. History is littered with lost opportunities, difficult challenges, pain and suffering, all because so many of us left unfulfilled Destinies when we died.

And so it is with Life. In every aspect of our society, when someone is missing and their Destiny is left unfulfilled, even for a day, our overall quality of life diminishes. Problems occur. Challenges go unmet. Opportunities are lost. Multiply that by the millions of people over the centuries that have "called in sick"—either out of ignorance or out of laziness—and you begin to understand how significantly the course of our collective lives is altered by Destinies that remain unfulfilled.

By what I witnessed through His eyes, I came to believe in real Destiny, in the specific sense of purpose with which we were all sent here, rather than in the fictional kind of Destiny portrayed in movie scripts and in the deeds of action heroes. I also received the answers I sought. There is, indeed, an earthbound Personal Destiny for everyone. There is enough purpose "to go around." And if enough of us fulfill our purpose, eventually even those in the world who are disadvantaged will acquire the capacity to fulfill their Personal Destinies too.

The Search

That vast world "office" soon vanished, and I began to see many people I know, though none were in Heaven at that moment with me. Through Christ's eyes I saw my daughter Laura, my cousin Diane, my wife Sally and my ex-wife Cindy, my mentor Steve, my co-workers Rose and Juan, a former fellow Toastmaster named Catherine, my high school best friend Bob, my friends Janice and Isabel, and many others living their lives on earth, searching for purpose. Some of those I saw are reading this book today. Janice and Steve have since passed away.

They were looking for what we all seek, at least in our dreams, even if we're unwilling to admit it publicly. They're in search of purpose and they want to do something with their life that is significant, meaningful and important to someone. Surveys of Americans almost always reveal that the thing we seek most is not more money, but rather, more meaningful work. Work that matters. Because we want to matter.

The fact is, we do matter. We matter to God, and He put us all here with a purpose. We all have a mission that is unique and personal just to us. A role to play in this life, impacting other lives in a way that no one else's role can. That role, personally designed by God, is our Personal Destiny. Some of us discover it, and fulfill it, during our years here on earth. We make the impact that God intended, and the world (or some piece of it) is a better place because we lived and worked and played here.

Most of us, though, never discover our Personal Destiny and, therefore, never fulfill it. Some of us find it, but never recognize it. Some of us look, but never find it. And, sadly, some of us simply don't believe in it, or don't care, and never even bother to look for it. Those people simply exist. They never really live.

Don't let that be you.

Finding & Fulfilling Your Destiny: Step Two

Many of us never seek out our Personal Destiny because we don't believe it's real. We don't believe that we were put here to accomplish something specific, something important, something that can't be achieved by anyone except us. Or we conclude that even if Destiny is real, unique and important, it must also be difficult to find, so we stop the search before we ever begin to look. Even if we believe we're capable of finding it, we often look around at others who are living fulfilled lives and convince ourselves that we don't have the talent and skill and intelligence to do the same thing. We don't have what it takes.

The second step in finding and fulfilling your own unique Personal Destiny is recognizing that Destiny is real *for* you, and unique *to* you, and that you have both the capability to find it and the skills and abilities and talents to fulfill it. Although you see yourself as an ordinary person, the capacity to do something extraordinary lives inside you at this very moment and will exist there as long as you are on this earth. It is critical to understand this because you'll never be successful searching for something that you don't first believe is real.

My Destiny Revealed?

At last, the time had come to learn why I had been allowed to make this amazing journey. Through His eyes, I saw myself in a meeting room in an office building in Plano, Texas. It was 2005 and several of those who worked in the building were streaming into the room for one of the Personal Strategic Planning workshops that I conducted for more than 2,000 of my co-workers in California, Texas and Arizona during my five years with Countrywide.

I always received great reviews after these sessions and still get notes and emails from those who participated, thanking me for setting them on a course toward a more meaningful life and career. One of the many talents I don't have, though, is the ability to read people's thoughts. I never knew what was on the minds of those in my sessions, which is probably a good thing because those who were daydreaming would have undoubtedly deflated my spirit.

But through His eyes, I actually had the opportunity to see into the thoughts of those in the room. I was amazed to find that most people were being re-energized and their passions were being reawakened as we talked about their mission in life and their vision for the future. The thought of actually doing what one was meant to do instilled feelings of excitement and anticipation in almost everyone; that is always my goal as a workshop leader.

While I was pleased to confirm that I achieved my goal, I received a special kind of fulfillment from the thoughts of a young underwriter named Vicky. Through His eyes, I saw that she found the session transformational. She determined early in the two hour session that it was the best use of her time in years. She soaked up every word like a sponge and made a commitment to change the direction of her life.

I never saw Vicky again and lost track of her many years ago, but I now saw the image of her in that meeting room dissolve into a gathering of senior citizens and disabled adults in a much larger room. In the middle of that group was a woman I recognized as an older version of Vicky. She was putting smiles on their faces, to match the big smile that was on her face. As I edged closer to her it was obvious to me that, in making life a little better for these people, she had found her calling. The twinkle in her eye was my first clue—and my ultimate reward—as I reflected back on all of the workshops I had led over the years.

We left Vicky and drifted back to a grade school in Illinois in 1961. After finishing lunch, my class had been dismissed to the playground; a kid named Mark and I were swinging on the monkey bars, burning off some energy before it was time to return to the building. We were talking about what we wanted to be when we grew up, a conversation I had long since forgotten and still didn't remember, even as I now watched. I wanted to be President, I announced proudly, knowing even at that young age what I would pursue for the next twenty or so years. Mark wasn't quite so sure. He loved solving mysteries and thought that being a detective might be fun, but he just wasn't sure.

At the time, Perry Mason was on television and my parents watched it all the time. I caught enough of it to know that he was a lawyer and that he solved mysteries. So I suggested to Mark that he be a lawyer, although I couldn't tell him what a lawyer was when he asked me. He said he might be a lawyer, but he'd have to ask his mom. The bell rang and we ran toward the school and into the anonymity of the next fifty years. I lost track of him after second grade when my parents moved and I went to another school, but after all those decades he was in clear focus once again. Sitting behind a cherry wood desk in a large Chicago law office, he was unrecognizable as the kid on the monkey bars but there was no mistaking his success as a trial attorney.

With Christ's help, it was becoming clearer to me now. My earthbound Personal Destiny probably has something to do with helping people find their way in Life. Through His eyes, I relived years of executive coaching, counseling co-workers on career paths, student advising while I was in college, management consulting, teaching college courses as an adjunct professor, tutoring high school kids in English, and teaching first grade Sunday school. Sometimes without even knowing it I've been coaching and counseling and teaching other people, literally since I was in grade school, and now I was finally beginning to understand why. I have the skills and abilities I need: mentoring, strategizing, speaking, organizing, writing, inspiring, analyzing, coaching, and planning. Recognizing that counseling is the intrinsic talent with which I was born, I was now about to be shown by the Son of God Himself how to use those skills and abilities to complete the ultimate counseling assignment . . . to guide you in the discovery and fulfillment of your own unique Personal Destiny.

As recess ended and I watched Mark and I head across the playground toward the school, I noted that this "counseling session" had taken place more than fifty years earlier. Wondering aloud whether I had enough time left in my life to fulfill a Destiny, I pointed out my rather significant health issues and the fact that I was turning fifty-seven years old, with a real age probably somewhere in the mid-seventies. Could I possibly have enough time left for this Destiny thing? He smiled softly and assured me that the pursuit of Personal Destiny is a journey, and it's never too late to begin the trip. He knew that those whose lives I will touch along the way were already encouraging me to begin now.

The Destiny Road

The school playground faded from view, and through His eyes I now saw a long stretch of lonely highway that seemed to dead-end at a mountain range a hundred miles in the distance. A solitary car was making its way along the road toward the horizon. I recognized both the car and the mountains from a trip I had taken four years earlier with my daughter Laura.

She had lived with me for a while after graduating from high school in the Colorado high country, but ultimately concluded that California living was not for her. She wanted to return to Colorado to go to college and I made the 1,000 mile trip with her so she could get her car and belongings to the college town of Greeley without having to do it alone. Now, years later, I was reliving the trip, watching as Laura and I left Interstate 15 in the middle of Utah and turned on to Interstate 70, headed east into Colorado. The road stretched out before us into an endless ribbon that we could see for miles. And miles. And miles.

On the horizon, hours in the distance, were the Rocky Mountains. Beyond them was our destination, Greeley. We couldn't see that destination, but we knew it was there. Laura knew where she was going, but had no idea what would happen in the years ahead once she got there.

Through His eyes, I watched the car disappear in the distance and realized that, just as the sand castle represented a lifetime of choices, the road is an allegory for the pursuit of one's Personal Destiny. He redirected my view from the road to the mountains ahead . . . toward the Horizon, that mysterious thing that always seems just out of reach. The Horizon represents Destiny itself, where the road—your journey of discovery—comes to an end. If you get off at one or more of the exits along the way and lose your focus and commitment, your Horizon will remain Undiscovered. But if you stay on the road all the way to the end you'll eventually reach that elusive Horizon and get a glimpse of the wonders that lie beyond it.

Of all of the trips you'll ever take during your lifetime, this particular journey will be one of the most important. The highway now stretches out before you. The Horizon is in the distance, in its reliable spot, awaiting your arrival. All that remains is to learn how to read the signs that will tell you how to get there.

3

Rules of the Road

Why do we exist, if not to make life better for others?

Florence Nightingale (1820-1910)
Creator of the nursing profession

The greatest thrill of my life was the day I became a father, November 26, 1986. It was the day before Thanksgiving, and I had an extraordinary reason to give thanks. That was the day my daughter Laura came into my life. From then on, I realized that it was no longer "all about me."

Parenting matures us in a way that nothing else in Life can. All of a sudden we're presented with a little human that lives, breathes, eats and *depends on us for survival*. And there is no instruction manual! Parenthood is an awesome responsibility given to us by God; it's a necessary responsibility because it readjusts our life's focus on selflessly meeting someone else's needs before meeting our own. Sadly, though, some parents never get that and then wonder why their family is dysfunctional. Some husbands (including me, many years ago) and wives never figure that out either, and that's where divorce comes from.

When my daughter was born, I had no idea that as she matured, I would grow along with her. In Laura's own little way, she gave me insight into why *I* had been born . . . a discovery that would not come full circle until The Day I Went to Heaven.

The Lady with the Lamp

As Christ continued to show me Life's lessons, one Christmas morning came into focus that I had long since forgotten. Laura was about five or six, so it would have been the early '90's. It was 6:00 AM and I saw myself awakened rather unceremoniously, after about two hours' sleep, as she came in and jumped on the bed. Her eyes sparkled and danced with pure joy and she was almost out of breath as she excitedly told my wife Cindy and I what she had just seen in the living room. She had asked Santa for a portable driveway basketball hoop and a "big girl bed," and they were both there. She was on cloud nine all morning and all I could think of was the all-nighter I had just concluded in order to put both of these things together, the missing parts I had to jerry-rig replacements for at 2:00 AM, and the big cut on my hand that came from an obscure encounter with a sharp part.

But through His eyes, viewing this scene now, the negatives melted away and I realized something that had eluded me that morning . . . that the greatest gift I received that Christmas, and in fact, in my life, was the fulfillment I got from meeting the needs of others. Scenes began to spill out of my life as I watched. I felt the peace that overcame the panic of my unemployment and empty bank account when I had dropped a check in the mail to the Union Rescue Mission a few years earlier. I felt the sheer inner satisfaction that came from taking two hours out of my young life to shovel the snow drifts off of an elderly neighbor's driveway and sidewalks, without pay and without even going to her door to let her know who had done it.

I saw that Saturday near Christmas in the mid 1960's when I was a Cub Scout. We had conducted a food and clothing drive to help a family that had lost their home in a fire. Several of us Scouts and our dads met them at the donated home in which they now lived. We had filled a caravan of cars with toys and clothes and food and cash and were now carrying dozens of boxes and bags into their house. The family was crying, and when we finished the parents hugged several of the dads, including mine. That day promptly passed from my young mind and hadn't come back to me until now.

It's surprising that I forgot this incident so quickly, because of something that occurred that Saturday that, to my knowledge, never happened again throughout the remainder of my life. My dad cried. My big, strapping, thirty-something, football player dad sat in the driver's seat of the car and was reduced to convulsive, uncontrollable sobs. I asked what was wrong and he dismissed it as not feeling well. Only now—only in this way—did I understand the magnitude of what happened that day.

Through His eyes, I learned something I never knew. My mom and dad didn't have a lot of money in the '60's and we lived very modestly. Yet my dad had written a large check to the family, in addition to the food and new clothes he and my mom donated. As he sat paralyzed by emotion in our car that day, my dad wasn't sick, or sad, or angry. He simply was experiencing, probably for the first time, that higher plane of personal fulfillment we are capable of reaching when we live a life of service. He bubbled over when we got home that day, excitedly relating to my mother how grateful the family had been and how good it had felt to give. Imagine, learning one of Life's greatest lessons from a Cub Scout service project!

We left my parents talking in the kitchen and through His eyes, I suddenly found myself in a school in London in what looked to be about 1860. Florence Nightingale was addressing an assemblage of nursing students and I was close enough to touch her, although she had no clue I was there. This was a special thrill for me because, as a history buff, I always wondered what it would be like to be in the same room with one of those larger-than-life characters in history that we have all only read about.

Florence Nightingale always believed that she was called to the nursing profession directly by God. On this particular day, she was sharing with her students the importance of their life's work, a God-given mission to care for and comfort the sick. Her message was heartfelt, inspiring and genuine, and she began her lecture with words I will never forget: "Why do we exist, if not to make life better for others?" In one short question, she had equated service to others with the reason we're all here.

Even though she was speaking to nursing students, I understood why Christ had brought me here. Her question transcended the mission of a nurse and had impact of a much wider scope than London and the 1860's. Known as The Lady with the Lamp for her work during the Crimean War, she was now illuminating something far greater than she could ever have imagined as she stood there gazing out at her students. Her words were the very essence of earthbound Destiny and were relevant for all of humankind throughout both days past and days to come.

I found my mind drifting off to picture a world where everyone awoke each day with a mission to make life better for others, rather than concentrating on making their own lives better. No one was in need. No one was angry, or in prison, or at war, or divorced, or sick, or sad, or bankrupt, or lonely, or corrupt. No one cried, or swore, or said hurtful things to others. No one was murdered, or abused, or forgotten.

Christ smiled and shook His head slowly as He watched me come to the realization that such a world is what God has wanted all along . . . a world devoid of sin because people have honestly sought forgiveness and have been saved by grace through their faith . . . a world filled with love because everyone has moved past sin to seek and fulfill the most important of earthbound Destinies, waking each morning with the sole thought in mind of doing specific things that day to make life better for someone else.

He could sense my giddy excitement as I discovered that serving others is not only the basic tenet of our Eternal Destiny, central to loving God and everyone He created, but is the basic tenet of our earthbound Destiny as well. I had heard my entire life that "it is better to give than receive" and to "love others as yourself" but now, knelt in worship before the Throne of God and enveloped in His Glory, I was learning how real those lessons truly are. After all these years, I was finally grasping what it meant to genuinely serve, how vital that is to a fulfilled life, and that real love is about more than just caring deeply about people I know. It's about serving and caring for everyone, including people I don't know and will never meet.

Now that the student was beginning to understand what the Teacher sought to impart, I once again found myself facing Christ. He could tell that I was anxious to reach my own Undiscovered Horizon now that a foundational piece of it had been revealed to me. Divine intervention had already taken me down a significant stretch of the road and my impatience in reaching the end was showing. Once again His eyes took control and put the brakes on my haste. There were no shortcuts here. Reaching the Horizon would take additional search and discovery on my part, with His guidance and direction. My Undiscovered Horizon would have greater meaning to me once I got there if I fully invested myself in the search and, more importantly, I would be better equipped to show others how to navigate the road if I had actually done it myself.

Sensing my anxiousness to continue down the road, He cautioned me that I first had to fully understand the rules that govern the Undiscovered Horizon in order for my search to be successful. Even in Heaven there was apparently no escape from rules, although I saw them as something different this time. Although rules always seem to imply involuntary participation on the part of those on whom the rules are enforced, these particular rules were a valuable roadmap that pointed toward the Horizon . . . toward successful discovery of the most important thing I would ever look for.

Christ reminded me of what I had seen, personally, through His eyes just a few moments earlier . . . the reality of inherent God-given Destiny. He called belief in that reality the **Elemental Rule**, because you can never find anything that you do not believe to be real in the first place. I knew from what I had seen that Destiny was not something that could be learned, acquired or created on my own. It was a gift directly from God, intrinsic to me—and to you—on the days we each were born.

The **second rule**, second in importance to the Elemental Rule, is that earthbound Personal Destiny is always about just one thing: service to others. That service is foundational to loving both those who are in your life and those you will never meet, and it is also an important part of glorifying God and of living a Christ-like life. I had clearly learned that lesson as I listened to Florence Nightingale and understood the significance of her words. If your Destiny, once you think you've discovered it, isn't about service to others . . . keep searching.

Snowflakes and Fingerprints

*Earthbound Personal Destiny is unique to each one of us. This **third rule** is why earthbound Destiny is called "Personal." Although Eternal Destiny is shared by all of us when we're born, earthbound Destiny is unique to each of us. No one else was born for the specific reason that you were born. You're different in a fundamental and compelling way. And so is everyone else. If your Destiny, once you think you've discovered it, isn't personal and unique to you . . . keep searching.*

Wherever you are right now, as you're reading, look around at everyone within your line of sight. If you're at home curled up on the sofa and no one else is around, then close your eyes and imagine you're at the mall during the holidays, in the midst of a sea of humanity.

Look into the faces of everyone you can see, whether they're the real people you can see across the room or the imagined shoppers you're observing at the mall in your mind. Now, think for a moment. What is it about each of these people that makes them different than *every other person* in your line of sight?

If you said their gender, think again. More than likely, you can see more than one man and more than one woman. Ethnicity?

Probably not, unless you've spotted the one person from Bhutan who has moved to town. Education? I'll bet you're looking at several MBA's, several people with high school diplomas and more than one stay-at-home mom who is now liberated from child-rearing and has gone back to college. You'll see more than one man with facial hair, and more than one woman with long hair. Half of the people will have kids in tow, or teenagers who don't want to be seen with them. Hobbies? While it's true that it will be a challenge to find two people in your line of sight with the same hobby, you'll have to admit that there are few, if any, hobbies pursued by only one person.

Actually, there is just one thing that makes you, or any of the people in your line of sight, truly unique among all of the people of the world. It's the one thing that defines your Destiny. The one thing that sets the stage for real, true happiness in your life. The one thing that can lead you to real fulfillment because it is the key to the meaning of Life. Yet sadly, most people never find that key, much less use it. And they die without ever fulfilling their unique Personal Destiny.

Every man, woman and child in the world is different than everyone else. Just like snowflakes and fingerprints, no two are exactly the same. The One Thing that makes us distinct is that we're all born already possessing a unique combination of skills, abilities, talents and interests that no one else on the planet has in that exact combination.

I know that scientists have debunked the idea that snowflakes are all different, so before I get swamped with emails pointing that out, let me acknowledge the fact that snowflakes do sometimes resemble the shape of others. Perhaps I should have called this section *DNA Strands and Fingerprints* because the point is that no two *people* are exactly alike. Given the popularity of *CSI,* that title would have had a higher level of "coolness" anyway.

Now, think about your individuality. No two of us possess exactly the same skill set. No two of us were born with exactly the same talents or abilities. No two of us are attracted to exactly the same set of hobbies and interests. Two people charmed enough with each other to get married are different. Those who hang out in the same peer groups in school are different. Even identical twins are different.

Why *are* people different? Why do we all have different combinations of skills, abilities, talents and interests? And when we do share a particular skill or talent with another person, it is always to a varying degree, or on a different level. Go up to any group of people and ask about their hobbies. While there will probably be some overlap, no two people will give you the exact same list. Ask about the classes in which they received the best grades with the least amount of effort. Undoubtedly, you will hear different answers from everyone. Ask about the articles in the newspaper or the blogs on the Internet to which they tend to gravitate. Again, each person is off in a different direction.

In this world, we're fond of lumping people into groups because they're just like everyone else in their group. Again, look around. Do all Bulgarians have exactly the same skills, abilities, talents and interests? Do all women? All gay people? All Republicans? All residents of these groups share one demographic factor in common, but it starts and ends there.

We're all unique. No one has the same combination of talents, skills, interests and passion that you have. No one has them in the quantities that you do, or at the levels that you do. And you're unique for a reason. By now—if you've read this far—you know why.

Be Willing to Lose It All

Through His eyes, I saw that earthbound Personal Destiny must require you to "put everything on the line." The **fourth rule** *is that Destiny requires the ultimate risk, and is the ultimate test of faith. Pursuing your Destiny is not for the faint of heart, but Life's greatest rewards always require us to have faith in something we can't see and to risk something, like security or money, that we hold dear. If your Destiny—once you think you've discovered it—doesn't test your faith or demand that you risk anything . . . keep searching.*

Five months after my journey to Heaven ended and I had recovered from the surgery, I was laid off by my employer, a major bank, as God was still at work equipping me for the pursuit of my Destiny. Seemingly, I had lost it all. Between a mortgage and consumer credit, I was in considerable debt and didn't have much money in the bank to weather a sustained period of unemployment. The road ahead looked pretty bleak. The economy was weak and I was approaching my fifty-eighth birthday without an MBA or technology experience in my background, both of which are essential to finding a comparable senior level management position in my field. I should have been concerned, but I wasn't.

Actually, my mega-bank employer had done me a huge favor. I had held a position of relevance, importance and value with my previous employer. When that company was acquired by the mega-bank I continued to have employment, but my duties disappeared because others in the bank's vast organization were already responsible for them. I was left to carve new duties out of the turf of others and struggled with that for three and a half years. I had a nice salary and a senior vice president's title, but my job was essentially irrelevant. My career had dead-ended, my self-esteem had been destroyed and it was clear to me that I was staying there for the prestige of an SVP title with a Fortune 100 company, a six-figure paycheck and the security that paycheck provided. None were consistent with fulfilling my Personal Destiny, or any other Destiny on this earth. My role was meaningless and I felt defeated and of no value.

I prayed for answers. Just when my wife and I concluded that, security or not, I had to leave for the sake of my mental and physical health, the layoff occurred and I received a package that would sustain me for several months. Executives at my level usually need a year or more to find another job. I wasn't sure the money, and my inadequate savings, would be enough. As I said before, I should have been concerned but I wasn't. The layoff had actually been an answer to prayer.

You see, I had experience far more valuable than anything I had acquired at that bank. I had been to Heaven. I had seen my life as it was meant to be lived, and I was ready for it. So I gave up the security, the money and the "prestige" (if there ever really was any). It was risky and scary, but my life is built on faith and I now know for certain that God has already charted my course and that I am on track to complete it. Everything happens for a reason and I was ready for whatever would happen next. My life was at a crossroads and whatever lay ahead would be dramatically different than anything I had done before. I was ready.

My last day in the office actually fell on a day when our entire work team had a video conference that linked co-workers in California, Texas and North Carolina. My departure was last on the agenda and my boss gave me a chance to speak. I shared my excitement, and fear, about the opportunities that were out there for me and shared a favorite quote of mine that seemed to sum up not only what I was feeling at the time, but my wish for their future as well. Christopher Columbus once said that "you can only cross the ocean when you have the courage to lose sight of the shore."

I have that courage. Appropriate to this rule, I call my courage Faith.

A few months later, I had the chance to test the risk part of this rule and once again Christ was there to guide me, even though by now my visit to Heaven was nearly a year into my rear view mirror.

After three years of emails from a book publicity guru named Steve Harrison, I had finally decided to respond to him and found myself attending his Publicity Workshop in March of 2012 in the ballroom of a Philadelphia airport hotel. It was two days of the most intense learning I had ever experienced. Steve's information was great; I learned a lot from him about how to be an author and about what it means to be one.

At the close of the Workshop, he offered an opportunity to be a part of a program he called Quantum Leap. The program is an intensive year designed to provide the participants with the opportunity to make a Quantum Leap . . . as authors, as spouses, as employees, as people. The cost was significant—at least in my world of unemployment—but would be reduced if I signed up before the Workshop adjourned that afternoon. I didn't have the cash, so I would have to max out my last credit card. Common sense told me not to do it, but I also sensed that this was something I needed to do in order to leave the Horizon behind and make significant progress toward my Ultimate Destination.

Since this would be a significant financial decision for us, I called home to ask Sally what she thought. After pondering it for a few moments, she asked, "Are you willing to lose it all to pursue your Destiny?" I was lost in thought, not sure how to respond. She followed up her question by saying "I am, because I believe in what you learned and saw in Heaven. I think you have a story that needs to be told. If this program can help you tell it more effectively and can help you more effectively share it with others, then I'm willing to risk everything on you."

I knew that by "everything," she meant the house, the credit rating, the rest of our savings and probably our sanity. The Workshop was on a break and there were people milling around everywhere. As I huddled on my cellphone and struggled to hear her in the middle of the din, she wrapped the conversation by saying, "If you're willing to lose it all, I am too. I have faith in you and will leave the final decision up to you." With that she said good-bye and the call ended.

My father and mother were raised during the Depression and valued security. They didn't take risks, and passed those values on to me. I don't gamble and have never done anything to risk the security of my future, yet this opportunity to take a Quantum Leap kept tugging at my psyche. Sally had given me permission to make a decision that I couldn't make without help.

I closed my eyes to pray in the midst of the noise and confusion of that hotel ballroom. Bowing my head, I began to think of what to say. Before I could utter a single word, I saw the face of Christ. He nodded gently and smiled. I had my answer.

So, I guess I am willing to lose it all. Willing to risk everything. Willing to stand on faith to fulfill my Destiny. In light of the reward, the risk is a small price to pay.

It's All About Focus

*Just as a road trip demands focus on the destination if you expect to get there safely within the timeframe you've set for yourself, the search for your Destiny requires focus as well. Through His eyes, I understood that your Personal Destiny trumps everything else in your life. Initially, you might think that there will be some exceptions to this **fifth rule**, such as your faith, family or career, but there are not. Since Destiny is God-given, faith is necessarily interwoven into it already. For most people, their job or career is central to their Destiny (although not synonymous with it), and family members generally play key roles in the fulfillment of Destiny. For example, my wife Sally played a significant role in the completion of this book, and will have a similarly important role when I begin speaking publicly in support of the book's message. If your Destiny—once you think you've discovered it—can't become the central priority of your Life for you . . . keep searching.*

Janet Nowicki, better known to fans of Olympic ladies figure skating as Janet Lynn, went to my high school in Rockford, Illinois and graduated a year ahead of me back in the early '70's. Every now and then, during times of the year when she was at school, I would pass the diminutive legend in the hallways between classes. Glancing over at her, I never ceased to be amazed by her tremendous focus.

She began skating at the amazing age of just 2½, probably not long after learning to walk! By the time Janet was just 11, she was the youngest skater to have successfully navigated the rigors of the United States Figure Skating Association. Two years later she won the US Junior Ladies Championship by landing a triple salchow, a jump that more experienced skaters rarely tried in competition. At 14, Janet was a member of the US Olympic team at the 1968 winter games in Grenoble, France. She finished out of the medals, but still came in 9th. From the late '60's through the early '70's Janet won five US championships in a row and a North American championship, among other honors. In 1972 she made a return trip to the Olympics, capturing the bronze medal at the Sapporo, Japan games.

Many experts in the skating world consider Janet to be one of the greatest freestyle skaters of all time, if not the greatest. In 1974, when she signed on to skate professionally with the Ice Follies, her contract made her the highest paid female athlete ever, at that time.

Janet always considered her talent to be God-given but it still took an incredible amount of focus to become an Olympic medal winner. It does for any Olympian, and for anyone else who fulfills Destiny. Hours of training, every day, often at times when many of the rest of us are still hugging our pillows. Years of self-imposed sacrifice. Years of focus, knowing that the ultimate payoff, even if it isn't a gold medal, will be worth it.

In spite of being a dominant ladies free style skater for several years, Janet never won an Olympic gold medal. She never could be as dominant in the compulsory figures, the key to winning any skating championship, because her short stature prevented her from surveying the ice as effectively as taller opponents could. She never stood on the platform with a gold medal around her neck, but Janet did fulfill what is most likely her Destiny.

In Sapporo in 1972 she was trailing after the compulsories and was out of the running for the gold medal even before the free skating began. As she sat in her room crying and praying, Janet decided to use her skating as a vehicle through which the love of God would shine on her audiences. He provided that opportunity early in her free skating program when something happened that was a rarity for Janet in a free skating program. She fell.

The audience held its breath for a few moments, heartbroken for her. When she looked up and into their eyes, the tears they expected were nowhere to be seen. Instead, her face blossomed into a broad smile. At that moment, everyone watching fell in love with her as she rose from the ice and glided off into skating history. Janet finished her program with such style and grace and class and intensity that she overcame both the fall and her rather average compulsory score to take a place on the podium as the bronze medalist.

With her smile and her classy approach to defeat and disappointment reverberating through the hearts of all who had watched her, Janet was ready to fulfill what had probably been her earthbound Personal Destiny all along. She became an inspirational speaker and author, and was a catalyst for transforming millions of lives worldwide. With a single smile during what seemed like her darkest hour Janet shone God's love in a way that no one else could have. She had truly become a champion, both on and off the ice.

Your opportunity to become a champion is waiting for you now. You've been in training for an entire lifetime. The time has come to step out on to the ice and stay focused. Don't forget to smile.

Destiny Is Not a Career Choice

Many of the books written about Destiny urge their readers to create their own Destiny and to chart their own course by searching for just the right job or career. Through His eyes, I saw that the pursuit of earthbound Personal Destiny is not about looking for a job or choosing a career. The **sixth rule** *is that Destiny transcends any job, any career, and any profession. It is an overarching role that you play in Life that encompasses every aspect of your very existence. Every choice you make, every action you take, every thought you think and word you utter is knitted into the very fabric of your Life.*

Destiny is not about what you do; it's about who you are. If your Destiny—once you think you've discovered it—seems to be all about your career and not at all about your life . . . keep searching.

Through His eyes I saw a quilt made from thirteen pieces of cloth sewn together, with each piece representing one of what He called the Elements of Life. Once sewn together, the pieces—the Elements—become a quilt that covers the Life that each of us is given when we are born. Your Personal Destiny is woven into every part of that quilt. Each piece drives your Destiny and, in turn, is driven by it.

I recognized the quilt as a composite of the same thirteen aspects of Life that had come to my mind years earlier when I was designing the Personal Strategic Planning class for my co-workers at Countrywide. Christ smiled as I remembered how brilliant I thought I was at the time for thinking of those thirteen aspects of Life. I now knew that He obviously had something to do with it!

These are the words that were written on the thirteen pieces of cloth. Those who have taken my Personal Strategic Planning class will recognize these as the same concepts (though not necessarily the same words) that I taught in the class.

- *Faith*
- *Principles*
- *Wellbeing*
- *Partner*
- *Children*
- *Service*
- *Knowledge*
- *Work*
- *Home*
- *Money*
- *Friends*
- *Family*
- *Rest*

Once you've discovered your Destiny, think about the role each of these Elements will play in it and the impact that your Destiny will have on each Element. Are you willing to make any changes needed in order to make your life compatible with your Destiny?

Faith: How will living your faith impact your Destiny? If you do not have a defined faith in your life today, how will your Destiny be a catalyst for faith to awaken in you?

Principles: What roles will your character, core values and reputation play and what changes will you need to make in them, if any?

Wellbeing: What changes will you have to make in your present health to accommodate your Destiny?

Partner and Children: Will your spouse and children be amenable to supporting your Destiny? If not, does the possibility exist that their view will change in the future?

Service: In what specific ways might you serve others while fulfilling your Destiny?

Knowledge: What continuing education, formal or informal, will be necessary to support your Destiny? Will you have access to the opportunities and resources you'll need?

Work: What career choice will be most compatible with your Destiny? In what ways could you adapt your current career to be appropriate to your Destiny without making a career change?
Home: How will your current home (type, location, etc.) support your Destiny? Will you need to move, refinance, downsize, etc.?
Money: How will your finances impact your Destiny? What changes will you have to make in your present financial situation to accommodate your Destiny?
Friends: Will your friends, neighbors and co-workers be amenable to supporting your Destiny? If not, does the possibility exist that their view will change in the future?
Family: Will your extended family be amenable to supporting your Destiny? If not, does the possibility exist that their view will change in the future?
Rest: What leisure activities, hobbies and interests will be most compatible with your Destiny?

If you've truly discovered your genuine earthbound Personal Destiny, none of the yes/no questions above will be answered with a "no." The remaining questions should all be answered in way that allows every Element of your life to peacefully co-exist with your Destiny, and to thrive in its presence.

Destiny Is Ultimate Fulfillment of Life on Earth

*The **seventh rule** is the payoff, ultimate fulfillment. Although many people see fulfillment as doing what they love, or doing what they're passionate about, or doing what makes them the most money with the least effort, real fulfillment far exceeds any of those. Real fulfillment is a lifestyle, a life transformation. You feel genuinely different when you're doing and thinking and being the person you were meant to be. You fall asleep every single night with the certainty that you were the person you needed to be, every minute of that day. If your Destiny—once you think you've discovered it—does not energize you and fill you with the passion and emotion described in this paragraph . . . keep searching.*

Ultimate fulfillment is discussed in greater depth in Chapter Eleven, "The Power in You," so all I will note here is that it is the seventh, and final, rule.

Finding & Fulfilling Your Destiny: Step Three

Sometimes when you take a vacation or another type of road trip in unfamiliar territory, you get lost because you misread the road signs. You get off at the wrong exit, or make a turn when you shouldn't, or pass your destination altogether. These rules of the road actually function more like road signs than rules. They keep you advised of your progress and help you ensure that you've arrived at the right destination. If your Destiny is unique to you, focuses on serving others, promises ultimate fulfillment, is bigger than any job, worth fighting for, and trumps everything in your life, then you've arrived. Your Destiny is genuine.

Reading the road signs correctly ensures successful completion of **the third step in finding and fulfilling your own unique Personal Destiny**: recognizing that Destiny once you find it. Many of us mistake passion and "doing what you love" for Destiny without filtering it through the tests of the Rules of the Road. Had I known those rules decades ago I would not have spent the first thirty-five years of my life pursuing a dream that I mistook for Destiny. I ended up wasting time, money, energy and focus on something that isn't even a part of my life today (my desire to be President). It was an expensive lesson but if you're able to learn from my mistakes and avoid making the same ones yourself, I've fulfilled my purpose here.

The road stretches out before you, you have the map in hand, and the Horizon is no longer elusive. It's time to head for the mountains.

4

The Five Keys

For we are God's masterpiece. He has created us anew in Christ Jesus, so we can do the good things He planned for us long ago.

Paul the Apostle (AD 5-AD 67)
Ephesians 2:10 (NLT)

Back in 1992, Gatorade aired a television ad featuring a host of young boys and girls sharing the basketball court with Michael Jordan, while the voices of children sang "I wanna be like Mike" in the background. And as I'm writing this particular passage, I'm following the online squabbles of adults who want to be like Oprah . . . competitors in a contest to host "Your OWN Show" on her cable venture, the Oprah Winfrey Network. The desire by some people to be like Oprah was so high that some of those in contention were reduced to arguing about whose online votes were earned fairly and about how poorly the contest itself was constructed.

Michael Jordan and Oprah Winfrey are great role models for America's youth (and for adults as well), as are many other athletes, authors, singers, actors, models, astronauts, moms, co-workers, neighbors, dads, composers, bosses, presidents, Nobel Prize winners and many other people whom we all spend the better part of our lives trying to emulate.

My dad was my hero. He was smart, made enough money to provide a comfortable life for our family, played football in school, was a community leader in many organizations, worked his way up to senior management at work and fathered three kids who never did drugs, got pregnant or went to jail. And he had a deep and abiding love for those kids. My dad was an Everyman, but he was my hero. I wanted to be like him.

The fact is, though, that while most all of us want to be like Mike or Oprah, or someone else, we never spend enough time during our lives just trying to be ourselves. Trying to be the person we were born to be. Trying to find and fulfill that one role in life that is uniquely ours, and no one else's. As much as we may aspire to be like Mike or Oprah, we can't truly be like anyone else because only Michael Jordan can ever be just like Mike. Only Oprah Winfrey can truly be the kind of talk show host and inspirational leader that she is.

Most of us spend a lifetime chasing someone else's success, trying to be someone that we weren't born to be, because we don't understand who it is that we *were* born to be. Our lives are constantly in transition and we often mistake that transition for fundamental change. In reality, the old saying, "The more you change, the more you stay the same" is true. Transition in your life actually defines the person you were born to be, *if* you understand the person you are today.

Life in Transition

Early in the writing of this book, a friend of mine asked why anyone would want to buy it. That question caused me to break out into a cold sweat because it had never occurred to me that no one would want this book. Every author naturally assumes that people will be interested in what they have to say. As I pondered this question, I began to see the people I thought would stop long enough during their journey through Life to put thirty bucks in my tip jar and take a book.

I told my friend that the audience is large and includes those who wonder why they're here, those who feel that something is missing but don't know what, and those who are happy—but not *really* happy. The audience also includes people who think they could contribute more than they do, people who want to make a difference, and people who don't like their life but don't know what else to do. And, of course, the audience includes those people who know there is something they're supposed to be doing but don't know what, as well as the people who simply want challenge, fulfillment, adventure, or a solution to life's mysteries.

But my friend pressed me further, wondering how I knew there *are* any people like that out there. I know there are, which is why her original question had taken me by surprise. One recent poll found that 20% of Americans are generally unhappy and another 26% are neither happy nor unhappy. Another showed that 55% of employees are not engaged in the work they do, and that fully 80% of the workforce plans to look for another job once the economy improves. The indexes that measure consumer confidence have been dismal for years. Other polls show spiritual fulfillment absent in a majority of respondents. I *know* there are people in need of this message. People who are bored, lost, resigned, confused, frightened, overwhelmed, unfulfilled. Still, she persisted. "But who *are* they?" she demanded.

That prompted me to make a list of the people who are *ready* to seek their own unique earthbound Personal Destiny. I made the list not so much to quiet her, but because I'm confident that you will see yourself, or someone you know, somewhere on it. If you do, you'll know that you made the right decision to read this book, or to give it as a gift to someone you love.

So . . . here is the list. Do you recognize yourself, or anyone you care about? Perhaps your life is in transition, or at a crossroads.

Possibly you've just graduated, have your entire life ahead of you, and are in search of adventure, discovery and meaning. Or maybe you've just retired, but you're not ready to *retire*. Perhaps you still have a job, but you're at a dead end because your career is disappearing or leaving you behind. It could be that you're in the ump-teenth year of an 8-to-5 office grind, or are a stay-at-home mom wanting more than a daily routine and conversation with a toddler. Maybe you're a Christian, but you still don't know exactly *how* you fit into God's Plan. Quite possibly, you've just experienced loss in your life—the loss of a child or a spouse, or a marriage, or a job, or a home, or your self-esteem—and you want to find some reason for soldiering on. Or perhaps you haven't experienced loss at all. You're happy, but you're not *happy*. You feel successful, but not *fulfilled*. You're looking for something *more*. Maybe you already believe in Destiny, but don't know how to find it . . . or perhaps you don't believe in it, but you're curious. Is this "Destiny thing" real, and is it the answer to the uncertainty that seems to fill your life day after day?

In the end, the real audience for this message is simply the person who wants to leave the world better off because they lived. I'm convinced that person is you. You're seeking real meaning in your life and you're ready to find it. The time for discovery is at hand and your *Undiscovered Horizon* is waiting. Step Four provides the set of keys that will get the engine running and take you there.

Finding & Fulfilling Your Destiny: Step Four

Identifying the point of our existence—the purpose that our particular life has on this earth—is difficult for most of us because we often live to a ripe old age without realizing that our life has a very specific theme and is channeled in one direction. We're not conscious of some, or perhaps even all, of the events that occur in our lives every day which point to our earthbound Personal Destiny, nor do we understand how those events work together to identify our purpose. We read books that limit our Destiny to what we're interested in and what we like doing, but I learned in Heaven that it is far more complex, and far more important, than that. Christ showed me Five Keys that unlocked the secret to discovering the specific reason each of us is here and I will share each of them with you in the next five chapters.

Understanding each of the Five Keys and the collective synergy that allows them to work in concert to focus your life and define your purpose is the **fourth step in finding and fulfilling your own unique Personal Destiny.** Awareness of the Five Keys and the roles they play in your life frees you to pursue your own calling so you don't have to waste time and energy trying to be someone else, someone you'll never succeed in being. If Life has left you bored, lost, resigned, confused, frightened, overwhelmed, or unfulfilled, understanding the Five Keys will drive the change that is so desperately needed in your life.

As Christ began to show me how we can discover our earthbound Personal Destiny, I realized that the moments ahead would be the most exhilarating part of my time in Heaven. The secrets to a truly fulfilling future on earth were about to be revealed to me, although I would come to see that you and I have known them all along.

A massive oaken door suddenly materialized in front of us, so large that I couldn't see either the left or right side of it. I didn't know whether it was the door to a room or to a building, but on the right-hand side of the door I noticed a large rectangular iron plate mounted with bolts. In the center of the plate was the largest keyhole I had ever seen. Just as it began to strike me as strange that any door in Heaven would need to be opened with a key, I noticed that Christ held an enormous arrow-shaped iron key in His hand. He would never need a key to open a door; I recognized that it was a symbol for the answers to the questions now swirling in my mind about how to successfully navigate my way to the Horizon.

He told me that this was the first of five doors through which we would pass, each to be unlocked with a different key. Behind each door I would gain a portion of the wisdom and understanding that I would need to reach the Horizon.

As He slipped the arrow-shaped key into the hole in what he spoke of as the First Great Door, it slowly swung open, revealing that my initial lesson was veiled within yet another panorama from my past.

5

Direction: The First Key

Your values become your destiny.

Mahatma Gandhi (1869-1948)
Indian political and social leader

Through His eyes, I saw myself working on my very first strategic plan in a cramped second floor office at The Commercial Bank in Salem, Oregon back in the mid 1980's. Although I didn't have a clue at the time, this project would launch me on a journey of nearly three decades in that profession. I was bent over a black metal desk, wordsmithing the Bank's mission statement. Just as a company's mission is shaped by the organization's core values, our own individual missions on earth are shaped by our own personal core values. Those values, in tandem with our mission, shape our vision for the future. In a business setting that is generally the senior management team's vision; for each of us individually, it is the fulfillment of our earthbound Personal Destiny once we have discovered what it is. Core values are critical.

He continued to give me a series of brief glimpses at my work in strategic planning over the years, developing plans for my employers and for my consulting clients, teaching strategic planning at the community college level and at the American Bankers Association bank marketing school, and giving keynote speeches and workshops on planning at business conferences for more than twenty years. As I watched, I was amazed that such a career had blossomed from reading a single article on the subject to prepare for a random work assignment handed to me many years ago by a CEO because no one else had time. Christ was quick to emphasize that nothing about my career in strategic planning had been random. I had been born with the tools I needed, in anticipation of one day writing this book and helping people as a part of fulfilling my Personal Destiny. Because planning is such an important part of fulfilling Destiny, He had given me knowledge I didn't even realize I had until that CEO handed me the out-of-the-blue planning assignment years ago. He told me I would use that knowledge again, to fulfill my own Destiny.

I wondered how planning could be so critical to Destiny and He prompted me to think about the elements of a plan. Whenever Christ would question me or prompt me to think of something, I always found myself looking through His eyes yet again. I learned what He already knew—and what I needed to know—by being a part of Him for a few fleeting seconds, viewing lessons I had already mastered during my lifetime without knowing they were preparing me for a much more important assignment.

In the blink of an eye, I was again gazing at myself telling audiences what was important about strategic planning. It isn't the planning process that is the most important part; it's the elements of the plan, core values in particular, and how they interact with one another to help an organization, or a person, realize their vision for the future. It now came together for me. Core values, shaped by our faith, are the foundation upon which our Destiny is built. I had been helping people define their own values in workshops for years. Now I knew why.

Core values are an enduring and constant collective set of deeply held personal beliefs, norms, standards and principles that guide your behavior, your relationships and your decision making throughout your life. They reflect your highest personal priorities relative to who you are and who you want to be, and they rarely ever change. Your core values define the direction of your life and shape your approach to living, feeling, thinking and doing. They impact—and are impacted by—the "life drivers" that will be discussed later in this chapter. Core values and life drivers work in tandem to influence every single decision that you make during the course of your lifetime. Even snap judgments and last-minute decisions are guided by your core values and life drivers. There are several hundred different core values, although experts maintain that the average person has only five or six. A few examples of that vast array of potential values include *Achievement, Faith, Security, Knowledge, Autonomy, Perfection* and *Power*.

Our values are so engrained in us that most of us have never made a conscious effort to think about what they are, or to sit down and actually make a list of them. When people ask us what our values are, we usually stumble and stutter or mention things that more closely resemble political views.

Suddenly, I realized that after years of teaching others about how to identify their own core values, I had never taken the time to define mine. Was now the time? Realizing that I was still knelt in worship at the foot of the Throne of God, I thought that there would probably be a more appropriate opportunity later. At that point I received some unspoken encouragement that the time was exactly right. I had just received The First Key . . . The Key of Direction. Instead of looking through His eyes, I was now looking directly into them as He drove an important point home: my values are the guiding principles that point my life in the right direction. Consciously being aware of what they are is a critical beginning to discovering my Personal Destiny, vital to making the right decisions for my life from this point forward. The loving eyes into which I stared became insistent and commanding. They underscored the importance of being in touch with my values and implored me to take their identification seriously.

In an instant, dozens of personal values began to flash before my eyes. Some were gone in an instant, while others lingered long enough to make an impression in my mind. He could sense that I was overwhelmed and comforted me with reassurance that my core values would become known to me soon enough.

Nearly forty of the three or four hundred words that flew through my brain made an indelible mark there. I could now see them all at once and some began to fall away on their own. I sensed that it was because they are not as fundamental to who I am as some of the others. This continued for an instant or two, until there were only six words remaining before my eyes. I glanced at Christ and His nod confirmed that these are the values that are core to my existence on earth.

Faith, Independence, Encouragement, Influence, Discovery and *Preservation* are my core values. I immediately recognized them as my essence. In concert with each other, they are me. *Strategic Perspective* and *Communication* had remained visible to me for a moment or two before disappearing, probably because strategic planning, public speaking and writing are what are what I do for a living. But they simply aren't inherent enough throughout the fabric of who I am. *Achievement, Knowledge, Intensity, Prosperity* and *Order* also lingered before my eyes for a while, but ultimately weren't among my core values either. While all are definitely a part of who I am, they simply don't define my spirit significantly enough to be core values.

Faith, Independence, Encouragement, Influence, Discovery and *Preservation*. Now, when someone asks me about my values, I'll know what they are and will be able to share them. More importantly, they're the first clues to my earthbound Personal Destiny.

Think about your own core values and what they might be. While they will not come to you in quite the same manner that mine did, the process for you will be surprisingly similar. You'll need to do a bit more of the heavy lifting than I did though.

In identifying your core values, it is helpful to have a copy of the *Your Undiscovered Horizons Personal Destiny Plan* workbook. In that resource, you'll find a menu of more than 280 common personal values and their definitions, arranged in alphabetical order, for your use in identifying the half dozen values that guide your life. Don't be overwhelmed by the list. It's comprehensive by design because it is intended to be an idea generator for you. Many of you, when asked to list your values on a sheet of blank paper, will probably have a difficult time thinking of even one without the benefit of the Divine Guidance that I had. Even if you are able to think of one or two, those might just be values that come to mind first, but those on your final list should be the half dozen or so that truly shape your life. Therefore, the rather exhaustive list in the workbook (or you can use a list of common personal values found through an online search with your browser) is provided not only to help you think of your values, but to ensure that you end up with a list of those that are truly your *core* values.

First, go through the entire list and circle those values that influence the decisions that you make during the course of everyday living. Don't worry about the number you're circling; just be certain that the values you are circling drive your daily decision-making relative to your career, family, home, faith, finances, health, leisure time, friends, community service and continuing education. Do not circle words that may describe you, yet do not generally influence your decisions. For example, I enjoy things that bring me pleasure and I often strive for punctuality, but neither of those values is central to who I am and what I do every day.

Do not circle values that you would *like* to have. For example, *Health* is not one of my core values even though I wish it were. I weigh 260 pounds and have a large belly. Although I'd like to weigh the 215 pounds that someone of my height (6'3") is supposed to weigh, I can't get there because I don't exercise enough and I eat too many sweets. If *Health* were a core value of mine, I would eat healthy, exercise regularly and change my lifestyle so that I could get rid of those unwanted pounds and lengthen my life. So, only circle values that are actually driving your life decisions *now*.

Next, look for values you circled that are similar to others you may have circled. For example, *Autonomy* and *Independence* are similar, as are *Money* and *Wealth*. In cases like this, choose the value that is most descriptive of who you are and how you make decisions. The values descriptions in the *Destiny Plan* workbook are a valuable resource in helping you decide which of similar values to choose. Eliminate all of the similar values that you ultimately do not choose, as they are no longer in the running for your core values list.

Next, re-read all of your circled values and cross out any that, in retrospect, are clearly not as significant to your decision-making process as others on the list.

Finally, make a list of the "surviving" circled values so that you now have them in a compact form and can study them more easily. Select the value from the list that has the **most significant** impact on how you live your life today, the value that most significantly defines who you are. From among the remaining values on your list, select the one that has the **next most significant** impact on how you live your life today. *Repeat* this final step until you have no less than four—and no more than six—core values.

Identifying your values is not easy, but nothing worthwhile is ever easy. This is a very important step toward discovering your Horizon. If you think about these values and what they mean, you should now be able to write a short profile that accurately describes the essence of who you are. Here's my attempt, based on my core values. This paragraph definitely captures the essence of who I am, a fact verified by my wife and close friends when they read it.

If you are acquainted with me personally, let me know if you think this paragraph describes me accurately:

"My greatest source of fulfillment lies in comforting, inspiring, advising, reassuring, mentoring, coaching and consulting those who need encouragement, guidance or counsel. I actively seek to be a center of influence in those areas in which I have significant expertise, and am exhilarated when I discover breakthroughs while learning or exploring. Although I value and appreciate transformational change, I consider the preservation and protection of culture, traditions and heritage to be vitally important. I believe in self-determination and self-reliance and like to live independently of control, limitation and supervision as much as I can, except where God is concerned. He is the highest priority in my life, and every day I strive to live as He directs me through His Holy Word."

What do you think? Write a similar paragraph based on the core values you just identified for yourself. If you've truly identified your *core* values, the paragraph will be a spot-on profile of you and of the essence of your character, and it will offer the first clue to your earthbound Personal Destiny.

When you've finished identifying your core values and writing your short paragraph, please consider sending them to me at JimMcComb@UndiscoveredHorizons.com. I'd like to follow you on the journey to discover your Destiny!

The latest visual tour of my strategic planning career came to an abrupt halt when I saw myself working late into the night for weeks on end, completing a major research project while a partner in the Centre for Strategic Management. I managed the Centre's Denver office until I was hired away by a client in California in 2000. We worked on that research project for two years defining what we called life drivers, which are inherent in every one of your core values and work in concert with them to drive every decision that you will ever make.

In our research at the Denver Centre for Strategic Management we learned that all human beings share five drivers that determine the way in which our core values shape every decision that we make in life. Where (and how) we live, who we marry, what we buy, where we go to church (and if we go), who we vote for, the friends we choose, the hobbies we pursue, the career we select, when we retire, the way we choose to parent our children (and whether or not we even choose to have them), how we handle money, what we eat, how we manage our health, where we go on vacation, the clubs we join, what we study in school and the charities we support are just a few of the decisions we make that are shaped by our core values and life drivers. In short, they influence every single thing that we think, feel, do and say.

As we studied how human beings make decisions, five common denominators—Hopes, Dreams, Visions, Fears and Aspirations—surfaced over and over in our research. One of these five, or a combination of them, drives every decision that you and I make. All of us have these common denominators woven into our core values, no matter who we are. They are predictors of the future, not merely explanations for the past.

Hopes are generally unfounded longings, desires or wishes that have no specific, real basis for fulfillment or realization in a person's life. People without a strong faith in God often succumb to feelings of frustration, failure and a lack of fulfillment when Hope fails to deliver. However, those *with* a strong trust in God who believe in the power of prayer and consider Faith and Hope to be synonyms can effectively negate the disappointment that may come in the wake of Hope when it fails to deliver. For them, God's will (as in the earthbound Personal Destiny with which He has gifted each of us) is always paramount and answers to prayer are therefore always contingent on His will.

Although Hope is generally viewed favorably by everyone in our society, unless it is faith-based it often arrests the potential of your core values (as opposed to aspirations) and can therefore be destructive to the fulfillment of your Personal Destiny. Life decisions based on Hope without Faith often fail to lead to the desired results and should be avoided. Those for whom Hope is the primary driver of their Core Values are often characterized by their high level of despair, pessimism and discouragement and are generally the *least* successful in life, as measured by their own standards. This can even be the case for some people whose Hope is Faith-based if they insist on using Hope as the basis for unrealistic or irrational expectations of God.

Dreams are fantasies, illusions and hallucinations that originate in the imagination. While Hopes often have no basis in fact, Dreams (as in daydreams, not those we experience while sleeping) are often logical extensions of some existing level of educational or career attainment. For example, a governor may dream of being President of the United States someday or a writer may dream of winning a Pulitzer Prize. Each of these dreams is fundamentally different from hoping that the economy will get better or that a relative with cancer will not die. Dreamers usually have lower levels of disappointment than those who Hope because they are less likely to count on a positive outcome. While Dreams are less likely than Hope to result in poor decisions relative to your core values, they still offer less potential for steering you on the proper course toward discovering your Destiny. Those whose decisions are primarily driven by Dreams are the risk takers and visionaries and inventors and entrepreneurs who successfully morph their dreams and ideas into new products, new technologies and new sources of jobs called small businesses.

<u>Visions</u> are anticipated views of the future usually based on strategies articulated in a plan that, when implemented, produces a desired future. Different than both Dreams and Hopes, Visions are more likely to be realized because of the action plans attached to them. For example, if you're an adult without a college degree you might have a vision of attaining a better job with more responsibility and higher pay. Your action plan might look like this: determine the career or position you would like to attain, determine the area school that offers the best education in that field and the most convenience relative to your current work schedule, apply to the school, arrange for financial aid and child care if necessary, set a deadline for graduation and determine class load needed to meet the deadline, set aside regular study time each week that is free of distraction, etc. As you can see from this example, there is a clear Vision of the future (a specific job in a specific career at a specific future date), a clear strategy (earn a degree in a relevant field) and a series of action steps that will lead to the degree and to a higher profile job. The Vision is more likely to have a positive impact on decisions relative to your core values than either Dreams or Hopes because you're taking action that methodically moves you toward a specific goal, giving it a much better chance for success. If you're primarily driven by Visions, you plan ahead and prepare for the future. You invest heavily in retirement plans, in college funds for

your children, in extra insurance for disasters like fires and storms, and in continuing education for yourself.

Fears are the easiest of the five life drivers to understand, and the most devastating to your Destiny because of the constraints they place on the potential of your core values. They are the primary source of emotions like alarm, distress, worry, concern, agony, uneasiness, apprehension, panic and anxiety. They are "what keep you awake at night." Life decisions made based on Fear are generally poor decisions that are often costly and usually made too quickly. If you're primarily driven by Fear, you do not enjoy life and second-guess most of the decisions you make, therefore handicapping your own success.

Aspirations are strong desires, intentions or ambitions. An Aspiration generally falls between a Dream and a Vision. It is a Dream with more intent because it involves ambition, and it is a Vision without a methodical action plan designed to take it to conclusion by a specific date. For example, if you move to Hollywood with aspirations of being an actor you don't necessarily have a specific plan of action, but your strong drive and ambition may result in success anyway because of your sheer perseverance. You keep networking and going to auditions and taking the initiative to be in the right place at the right time. If you're driven by aspirations and ambition you do whatever it takes to be successful, in spite of not having a plan of action. Sometimes, your actions may not always be legal, moral or ethical in order to achieve the object of your desire. You may leave a trail of angry and hurt people in your wake on the way to success. Although you enjoy the highest degree of what you define as success, if your life decisions are driven by Aspirations you should use caution because core values—and, therefore, Destiny—are easily compromised by blind ambition. Caution is generally most appropriate if you aspire to high profile roles like CEOs, politicians, professional athletes and entertainers. If you aspire to a service role, like a teacher, a nurse, a police officer, a firefighter or a missionary, you'll probably not need to exercise much caution because people pursuing roles like these eventually become driven by Vision and base their life decisions on a plan (usually built around educational goals) rather than on ambition.

Life drivers work hand-in-hand with your core values to chart your course in Life, and complete the First Key to discovering your Horizon . . . The Key of Direction.

Through His eyes, I saw my core values in front of me: Faith, Independence, Encouragement, Influence, Discovery and Preservation. I also saw the patchwork quilt with the thirteen Elements of Life stitched on it. He was prompting me to ponder two more questions. How do I make life decisions every day? What impact do those decisions typically have on each of my core values?

He clearly wanted me to understand that allowing myself to be driven by any one of the things that I had defined as "life drivers" was OK. In spite of the conclusions my research had produced (that Visions were usually the preferred way to make decisions), any one of the five drivers might actually be appropriate, depending on the decision and on the core value to which it was related. That was a revelation for me. As a strategic planner, I had always been predisposed to the pre-eminent value of Vision. He smiled as I realized that Hope is not always a bad driver. That's why Faith exists. There are other times when Fear is an appropriate driver because it raises the flag of caution. Dreams are necessary because, without them, innovation and creativity never have a chance to work and bold new ideas wither and die before they even become thoughts. He also inspired me to re-think my conclusions about Aspirations since, as I have already noted relative to people like nurses and teachers, Aspirations aren't always bad. Many times they are a gift directly from God.

Think now about your own process of making life decisions, about what drives them, and about how they relate to your core values. Jot down any immediate thoughts you have, as you will need to refer to them as you go about the process of defining your Destiny.

Which of the five life drivers—Hopes, Dreams, Visions, Fears and Aspirations (select at least one, or as many as all five)—characterize the way you make decisions in each of the thirteen Elements of your Life? How do those life drivers impact the ways in which of your core values shape the direction of your life?

The answers to these questions are an important part of leading you to your Destiny because they help you understand the relationship between your life and your values. They also clarify the effect that your life decisions may have on your ability to discover, and fulfill, your Destiny because of the impact those decisions have on your core values.

What drives the decisions you make in your life? Drop me a note and let me know at JimMcComb@UndiscoveredHorizons.com. I'm traveling along with you on your journey!

6

Attraction: The Second Key

*Your imagination is your preview of
Life's coming attractions.*

Albert Einstein (1879-1955)
Theoretical physicist

Christ produced a second key. Unlike the first, this key was in the shape of a book. As before, He used it to engage the lock on the Second Great Door. Through His eyes, I now saw myself as a young boy of three visiting that grand old Queen Anne house on North Rockton Avenue in Rockford, Illinois. It was built in the shadow of the Civil War and had been home to three of my maternal grandmother's unmarried siblings since before the twentieth century began. Their father, Byron Woodring, also lived there with them (his wife had died in 1946) and I was nestled in his lap. It was in the waning days of December 1957 and we were visiting for Christmas from our home in Janesville, Wisconsin. He and I were in his favorite chair in the bay window in the dining room and he was reading from The World Almanac.

He would get the almanac every year and read it cover to cover. On this visit I sat and listened, riveted, as he told first-hand stories from his memories of the historic events that were recorded in the almanac. Since my days as a toddler I have always been fascinated by American history and stories of the past, but as I grew up I never really knew why. My great-grandfather had been reading from his brand-new 1958 almanac, and when he saw my amazement at the stories that lay inside that book he gave me his old 1957 edition as I left with my parents that day. They looked puzzled. After all, I was just learning to read children's books and in no way could have tackled an inch-and-a-half thick volume with phone book sized type and no pictures. Through His eyes, though, I saw the look of stunned amazement on my parents' faces a few months later as I taught myself to read using the 1957 World Almanac.

I never received another book from my great-grandfather, as he died in the fall of 1958 before the next edition came out. Now, more than fifty years later, that volume is a cherished centerpiece in what is the largest collection of World Almanacs in the United States. Beginning in 1958 I had asked for an almanac for Christmas every year, a tradition that continues to this day. About ten years ago I began seriously collecting those editions that had been published prior to my prized 1957 book. Today, I have every year, going back to the inaugural publication of the book in 1868, except for a few years in the late 1870's and early 1880's when publication was suspended.

As my great-grandfather faded from view, I wondered what the almanac could possibly have to do with anything. No sooner had that question crossed my mind than Christ answered it, showing me that an understanding of history and its lessons and consequences is important for anyone who plans the future. For the first time in my life, I now understood that my fascination with the past—something I had first been aware of as a toddler—was an *interest I had been given at birth. It was an interest that, unknown to me, had shaped my career as a strategic planner . . . an interest that had become an essential clue in identifying my Destiny.*

I now saw myself a few years later, in the spring of 1968, seated at a large round table in a huge hotel banquet room in Rockford, Illinois, where my family lived at the time. At the table with me were three other eighth graders and their parents, and my junior high English teacher, Miss Josephine Mathews. My parents were nowhere in sight and I was the only student in the room that night who was there with my teacher. A year and a half earlier, I never would have seen this evening coming.

As a seventh grader, newly arrived at Theodore Roosevelt Junior High School, I was a holy terror. A smart aleck. A cut-up. A troublemaker. The class clown. I was an anonymous face in the crowd, looking for attention. Throughout life, I have never been one of the "popular people." You know, the football player/cheerleader/class officer crowd. So in the fall of 1966 I was seeking recognition in other ways. I was a pimply-faced, nerdy-looking kid in search of an identity. I chose to seek it by acting out and acting up. Corporal punishment was still legal in those days and the male teachers and the vice principal used it liberally. In seventh grade I began a stellar career that earned me more than two hundred stinging swats with the paddle by the time I departed for high school in 1969. It still may be a school record.

Miss Mathews was a formidable adversary. In her early sixties, never married, a grizzled veteran of more than forty years of teaching, she had been at Roosevelt when my mother went to school there in the 1940's. She ruled her classroom with an iron fist and demanded that learning actually take place there. We obviously collided on the very first day and my entire seventh grade year in English was a nightmare, although I consistently earned A's and B's in class. When I drew her as my eighth grade English teacher, I thought for sure that God had designed His own unique brand of Hell for me. Little did I know that it was actually quite the opposite.

After Christmas, Miss Mathews gave us an assignment to write an essay titled, "What Being an American Means to Me." By now, my interest in American history and in politics was in full gear and I took off like a rocket on this assignment. I got an "A" on the essay, bragged to my friends and family, and thought no more about it. A few weeks later, Miss Mathews asked me to stay after class for a few minutes. As I prepared to be sent to the vice principal's office yet again, this time for some unknown transgression, she surprised me with news that she had entered my essay into a citywide contest for junior high school students. My work had won second place in the entire city, the second largest city in Illinois! I was ecstatic, and yet stunned. I loved to write. It was a hobby, but I never thought I had any particular talent for it.

She told me there would be a citywide awards banquet in a couple of weeks and that all of the kids whose essays had been entered were invited, along with their parents. As the day of the banquet grew nearer, my parents each had disappointing news for me. My mother was in the hospital having back surgery and would not be home in time for the banquet, and my father would be in New York on business for his employer, the Rockford Newspapers. My grandfather lay dying of Parkinson's disease in a local nursing home and my grandmother couldn't go because she would be watching my younger brother and sister. There was no one to take me.

My mother suggested that I ask Miss Mathews to go with me since she was the one who had entered me in the contest. Our relationship was still a bit contentious, but I knuckled under and asked her at school the next day because I wanted to be at that banquet to get my ribbon. She smiled, said she would go and, as I left the room, I saw her dab her cheek with a tissue.

So there I was at the banquet, the only kid with a teacher. The only one there without parents. As my name was called out as the second place winner, I arose and wound my way among the tables where several hundred people were seated. Just as the third place winner had been asked to do a few minutes earlier, I was invited to introduce my parents to the crowd. I briefly explained where my parents were and then introduced Miss Mathews as my teacher, adding that I would not be there had it not been for her. That part of the introduction had been totally unplanned; it just popped out *of my mouth as if the words had been divinely placed there.* As she arose to acknowledge the crowd, I felt an immense burst of pride that she had been the one to accompany me that night. She sat down amid the most thunderous applause of the evening, and once again I saw her put a tissue to her face.

During my entire time in Heaven, watching my life replay through Christ's eyes, I only touched one person. Miss Mathews. Once she was seated and my eighth grade self had returned to the table, I slipped in between the two of them and gave her a thank you hug. She shuddered a bit, but never knew I was there. Watching that banquet replay for the first time in more than forty years, I realized that Miss Mathews had been put in my life to turn it around and to get me back on the path to discovering my purpose. I also recognized that I had just played a role in the fulfillment of her Destiny. She retired a couple of years later secure, I believe, in the knowledge that her lifetime of teaching had left the world a better place.

During the three years I had Miss Mathews as an English teacher, she got me involved in the Optimist Oratorical Contest and the Roosevelt school newspaper, Teddy's News. I still have a roomful of trophies from my years in that oratorical contest, as well as additional trophies from more than thirty years in Toastmasters and tens of thousands of dollars earned during two decades as a paid pubic speaker. In ninth grade I was named editor of Teddy's News, *determining what the entire school read every two weeks and attaining a place in the student hierarchy that none of the popular kids ever reached.*

Most importantly though, as I say in the dedication to this book, Miss Mathews was God's hand . . . guiding me toward my purpose before I even knew I had one. Public speaking, writing, and critical thinking are all at the very heart of discovering my Destiny today. She taught me how to harness my interests and hobbies. She was my Pathfinder.

Christ went on to show me a myriad of other instances in my life when I was unconsciously attracted to interests, hobbies, articles, conversations and points of view that relate to my core values and were seeds planted in me before I was born, clues to the *purpose I was created to fulfill. Just as core values and life drivers are signs posted along the road that leads to the Horizon, so too are our passions and pastimes.*

Demographers tell us that the average American has between seven and nine true hobbies, pastimes and interests. Most of us, however, would have a tough time thinking of all of the things we're interested in if we were ever asked. I still add interests to my Facebook profile that I forgot to list and periodically remove things that I eventually realize I'm really not that passionate about. I did the same thing when I was single and had an online dating profile.

If there is anything in my life besides bills that I have too many of, it is probably interests. My attention span flits from one priority to another, from one interest to another, from one curiosity to another and I'm sure the same is true for many of you. Amidst the clutter of our lives, though, there are a few interests that are truly important . . . passions we have that take top priority whenever we have a spare moment, and sometimes even when we don't. Those passions are The Second Key to discovering your Horizon . . . The Key of Unconscious Attraction.

While I was in Heaven, Christ had emphasized the important role in my Destiny played by the interests to which I am unconsciously attracted. I knew the things that held the greatest interest for me but had a nagging desire to be sure I thought of everything. While I was recovering at home from my surgery, I did some thinking about the hundreds of hobbies and interests and passions and pastimes that exist out there. After a bit of time surfing online I came up with these general categories of hobbies, interests, passions and pastimes, and a few examples in each area.

Arts & entertainment: music, theatre, dance, magic/illusions, attending cultural events, listening to music, watching movies, watching television

Communication: writing, journaling, social networking, public speaking, reading, talking, animal communication, hypnosis & ESP

Raising or growing something: gardening, bonsai, showing dogs or horses, tropical fish, pets

Sports & games: playing competitive sports and games, playing non-competitive sports & games, playing table & board games, watching sports on television, gaming, playing video games, coaching youth sports

Collecting: collections, memorabilia, bird watching, photography, people watching, dining out (collecting "food experiences")

Creating/restoring/decorating: painting, woodworking, scrapbooking, restoring cars, cake decorating, home improvement, lapidary, cooking, sewing, home movies, home business, interior design

Learning: history, astronomy, foreign language, weather, geology, current events, gadgetry, science, travel, crossword puzzles

Family: genealogy, children's activities (sports, dance, piano, karate, etc.), time with grandchildren

Technology: computer programming, surfing the Internet, consumer electronics, amateur radio

Health: dieting and weight loss, working out, self-improvement, health foods

Causes: political, social, environmental, economic, faith-based, youth, charitable

As I looked at the list, I wondered if the pastimes I spend time on would be greater or less than the number of interests of the average American. Since I collect everything under the sun, I knew that would depend on whether collecting counted as one interest or not. I scanned the categories, and the more exhaustive list within each category that is included in the *Your Undiscovered Horizons Personal Destiny Plan* workbook. These are my interests, and the core values they support:

- Watching movies, in the theater and on television—*Discovery*
- Writing books—*Faith, Independence, Encouragement, Influence, Discovery, Preservation*

- Motivational / inspirational public speaking—*Faith, Independence, Encouragement, Influence, Discovery, Preservation*
- Social networking—*Encouragement, Influence, Discovery*
- Watching competitive sports, in person and on television (Denver Broncos, Los Angeles Angels of Anaheim, New York Mets, Tennessee Volunteers football and women's basketball)—*Discovery*
- Collecting (political campaign memorabilia, national park quarters, Hard Rock Café pins, Disneyland pins, baseball cards from the 1960's, books, historic newspapers, World Almanacs, toy tanker trucks, Broncos/Mets/Volunteers memorabilia, Little House on the Prairie porcelain dolls, autographs)—*Discovery, Preservation*
- Home improvement & decorating—*Preservation*
- Studying American history, politics and current events—*Discovery*
- Sudoku's and crossword puzzles—*Preservation* (of my brain)
- Surfing the Internet—*Discovery*
- Self-improvement—*Faith, Independence, Discovery*
- Reading the Bible—*Faith, Discovery, Preservation*

Twelve interests made my list. Since writing and public speaking are now my vocation rather than mere interests, they could come off the list. The remaining ten bring me to close to being in line with the number of interests an average American pursues. As you'll see, each interest supports one or more of my core values. Christ had told me this would be true, because passions and pastimes are predictors of Destiny as well.

None of these are interests I can remember acquiring on a specific day or even in a specific year. They were all inherent in me when I was born, and became known to me at appropriate times over the years. Now, to be fair, I should acknowledge that several of my interests, including the Internet, the Mets, the Angels, the Broncos, 1960's baseball, Disneyland, the Hard Rock Café, national park quarters and social networking, had not yet come into existence when I was born, although in every single case—except the Angels (I married an Angels fan)—the interests just came to me as those things came into existence. My interest in them never had to evolve; it was inherent in me from the very beginning. By the way, in case you were wondering, the answer is *yes*. The Bible had, in fact, been completely written by the time I was born.

As you reflect on your own passions and pastimes, I should explain the relationships between my core values and my interests so you will see how to relate your own interests to your values. I looked at each of my interests, one at a time, and asked myself how it was reflected in each of my six core values. As you scan my list, you'll notice that writing and public speaking are reflected in all six. Once I determined what I should be writing and speaking about, I knew that those activities would become my new vocation and would be at the heart of my Destiny. In November 2011 I left the corporate world behind to finish writing this book and to return to motivational speaking, a career that family issues had interrupted years earlier.

Writing and public speaking each support all of my values because I write and speak directly from my heart, which supports *Faith*. My writing and speaking bring an income and an inner peace that comes directly from a product I produce myself, freeing me from the control of an employer and supporting *Independence*. The content of my book, and of articles, speeches and educational content I've written and delivered over the years, is always intended to provide guidance and inspiration to those who read it (*Encouragement*), and to establish me as someone with whom people want to talk about this subject (*Influence*). Since I never write anything, or deliver a speech, without learning something new about myself, my writing and speaking support *Discovery,* and support my *Preservation* value because they preserve my thoughts and ideas for posterity.

I generally watch both competitive sports and movies with friends and family, and inevitably learn something new (*Discovery*) about them, and myself, as we banter during the course of the game or fellowship before and after the movie. That discovery strengthens our relationships. Knowledge acquisition also supports *Discovery*, as in the case of both surfing the Internet and studying American history and current events.

Home improvement maintains the value and beauty of our home and yard, supporting *Preservation*, while that same core value is supported in a different way by my daily ritual of completing the crossword puzzle and the two Sudoku's that appear in each issue of *USA Today*. I once read that mental exercise is believed to keep Alzheimer's disease and dementia at bay as people age and I'm taking no chances!

Social networking is viewed as mindless by many people my age, but I find it to be an invaluable source of business contacts (*Influence*), long-lost friends from school and past jobs (*Discovery*) and an opportunity to connect with people on their birthdays or at times when they're in need of prayer or an inspiring word (*Encouragement*). Reading the Bible is obviously deeply connected to my *Faith*, but I also find that every time I read it, I see something there that I haven't noticed before (*Discovery*) and because it helps me keep my values intact every single day I feel that it definitely supports *Preservation*.

My collections protect valuable artifacts from the past, some as old as 225 years, and when studied they offer a window to years gone by, supporting both *Discovery* and *Preservation*. Finally, the efforts I make at self-improvement every day support three of my six core values: *Faith*, as I work to live a Christ-like life; *Discovery*, as I constantly learn about needed improvements in some aspects of my life while celebrating successes in others; and *Independence*, embodied in the freedom my spirit enjoys when I live life as it was intended.

What are your passions and pastimes? Take a look at the eleven categories of interests, hobbies and passions. If you have the *Destiny Plan* workbook, examine the more exhaustive list included there. As you look through each category, ask yourself if you have an interest in anything that might be included in that category, whether I have listed it or not. Don't develop a list of two hundred items. We all have passing interests in many things, but only have sustained, passionate interest in a few things because we have limited time, money and energy to invest in them. That is the benchmark here. What have you spent time, money and energy on, regularly, for at least the past year or two? Regularly means that you invest yourself on a continuing basis in that hobby or pastime, and that you have most likely engaged in doing it at least once in the past month. For example, I love to read for pleasure but I only get sporadic opportunities to do it so reading didn't make my list. I've done everything on my list in the last two weeks, except collecting. I would have done that, too, except I missed the chance to add to my autograph collection at a gathering of Hollywood celebrities last weekend because I was in a cabin in the woods working on this book.

Check your list. If you have more than a dozen items on it, you're probably including things you don't make a significant investment of time or money in on a continuing basis. Once your list is set, evaluate each interest relative to your core values. Which value(s) is/are supported by each of the interests on your list, and why do you feel that way? In what way are they supported? Answering these questions honestly is critical because you're gathering yet more signs as to what your Destiny might be. You now know my passions and pastimes . . . why not send me yours? I'd love to know a bit more about you!

7

Opportunity: The Third Key

*When one door closes, another opens;
but we often look so long and so regretfully
upon the closed door that we do not see
the one which has opened for us.*

Alexander Graham Bell (1847-1922)
Scientist, inventor, engineer

Christ produced a third iron key, in the shape of a human face that I didn't recognize. As He guided the key into the lock to reveal what lay beyond the Third Great Door, the visions of Miss Mathews, and of my passions and pastimes, vanished and I now saw myself paging through the classified ads in the Denver Post, looking for a job. It was a scene I had long since forgotten, until my eyes focused on a particular ad. A nationwide consulting firm was interviewing, and would be at the Embassy Suites out by the old Stapleton Airport at the end of the week.

As anyone knows, networking is the key to finding a job. I had been working my network, but it was a slow, painful process. In spite of the fact that I already had a job, money was tight so I needed some immediate results. I never looked in the paper for jobs, and hadn't done that since the early days of my career. But for some unknown reason, I did it that day.

As I rummaged around in my brain searching for a reason why I might have decided to check the paper on that particular day, His eyes suddenly fast-forwarded to the week's end and I was watching a less-than-confident Jim McComb nervously navigate a job interview. Miraculously, I got the job and went all over the western United States and Canada on consulting engagements. While I've always loved consulting, in this job I often had the opportunity to do something more . . . something that energized me more than anything else ever had, even though I had never been taught how to do it.

Business owners and senior executives began to seek my advice and counsel on matters that were more personal to them, beyond the scope of any consulting engagement. Quickly, I found myself assuming the role of an executive coach, without any formal training, or even much knowledge of what an executive coach was. The role simply materialized out of nowhere, as a result of chance encounters I had with people I would never have met if I hadn't looked in the classified ads that day.

The firm had an executive coaching division and I often dreamed of being a part of it. Coaching exhilarated me, I was good at it (or so those who sought my counsel told me) and I longed to do it full-time. A few months earlier my eighteen year marriage had ended and my thirteen year-old daughter wanted to live with me, which wasn't the best scenario for a parent who traveled six days a week. The coaches didn't travel, worked out of home offices and coached full-time. It was a dream come true. I wanted, and needed, that job, but there were no openings and turnover in those positions was virtually non-existent. Then it happened.

I had been with the firm for about a year when I got a call from the Chicago home office while I was consulting at a large furniture store in Salt Lake City. One of the coaches had just died of a heart attack. He had a full complement of twenty five clients who were now, abruptly, without a coach. The next morning I was in my home office in California, with a headset and twenty five coaching clients. Improbably, I was now a full-time executive coach, drawing on my years of experience in management consulting and senior leadership, and doing something that truly fulfilled and energized me. Over the years, I went on to receive dozens of letters and emails from coaching clients to whom I brought immeasurable value.

Because I was in the right place, at the right time, I was now doing the Right Thing, all because I had decided to do something I never do. I checked the classified ads that day.

Think for a moment about how truly random Life is. You meet new people, learn new things, and encounter new challenges and opportunities every single day. The randomness occurs when you realize how significantly your day changes if you simply do one thing differently. You decide to check the job board of a company you'd like to work for, even though you have a job. You take your child to school instead of going straight to the office this morning. You go out to lunch today instead of brown bagging it and eating in the office lunchroom. You decide not to go to the doctor to have her check that nagging sore throat you have. You stop off to buy a lottery ticket at a convenience store, even though you never buy them. You decide to mow the lawn this morning instead of tomorrow afternoon.

Let's say you do the things I just mentioned above. You notice a dream job and the hiring manager is someone you have worked for in the past and know personally. You see a couple of other parents at school in the parking lot and begin to chat about some education issues that upset all of you; they ask you to run for the school board. You bump into an old co-worker at the sub shop you've gone to for lunch and discover that you're both now single; you set a dinner date for this weekend. By skipping the doctor, you eventually discover much later that you have cancer of the esophagus and it doesn't look good. Your lottery ticket pays off, and you decide to pay off your mortgage. While mowing the lawn, you finally meet the new neighbor who moved in three months ago and is never around; she turns out to be a financial advisor and ultimately begins managing your investments and makes you a ton of money.

Each of these scenarios actually happened to me, or a member of my family, or a co-worker or friend. What if one or more of them had happened to you? What if you had chosen to do those things five minutes earlier, or two hours later, or the next day, or not at all? Your chance encounters and coincidental opportunities would have changed. Your day would have changed. Your life would have changed, and discovering your earthbound Personal Destiny would be closer than ever. Or, perhaps, that Destiny may have been lost forever.

Generally, there are reasons you make the choices you do. We'll discuss those reasons more fully when we look at The Fourth Key, but for now I'll just say that you make those decisions because you're destined to make them. Your core values, life drivers and passions & pastimes have hardwired your Destiny into your decision-making, with occasional—and sometimes costly—exceptions. Again, we'll discuss those exceptions when we examine The Fourth Key.

Life is filled with those chance encounters and coincidental opportunities. Some you recognize at the time as being significant, but you don't recognize many others and that undermines your ability to easily discover your Personal Destiny.

Chance encounters are unplanned meetings or contacts with people who are specifically placed in your life by God, even though they seem to cross your path for no apparent reason. Over time, these people have significant impact on the direction your life takes in one or more of the thirteen Elements of Life. Often you don't recognize the significance of that impact until much later, if at all. Even when you do recognize the significance, you seldom connect it with your life's purpose.

How about coincidental opportunities? They're the chances to get closer to your Destiny that you do not actively seek or plan for because you often don't even know they exist. Like chance encounters, they seemingly drop into your life for no apparent reason. Over time, they have significant impact on the direction you take in one or more of the thirteen Elements of Life. Again, like chance encounters, you often don't recognize the significance of that impact until much later, if at all, and even when you do see it, you seldom make a connection with your life's purpose.

Chance encounters and coincidental opportunities are the Third Key . . . The Key of Opportunity. They show themselves in all thirteen of the Elements of Life. You encounter people in every Element that you never planned to meet, yet they ultimately make an important difference in that part of your life. You also encounter opportunities in every Element that you never planned to pursue, yet they, too, ultimately have a vital impact on that part of your life. As I saw through Christ's eyes, it is important to the search for our earthbound Personal Destiny that we recognize these people and opportunities when they come along and that we understand *why* they came along.

You can perfect your ability to recognize and understand by starting with what you already know. Within the context of each of the thirteen Elements of Life think about those people and opportunities that you now see as significant, even if you might not have recognized their importance at the time they occurred in your life.

Specifically, what long-term, sustained impact did these people and opportunities have on the direction that your life has taken? What real, lasting difference did they make in your life? How did you meet the people? Under what circumstances did those chance encounters take place? How did you receive the coincidental opportunities? What circumstances brought them about? What do these people and opportunities, and the circumstances under which you came upon them, have in common? Which of your core values, life drivers and passions & pastimes played a role in the impact that each of these people and opportunities had on your life? Do you notice a common theme?

Through His eyes, I saw countless examples of chance encounters and coincidental opportunities that I had experienced throughout my lifetime. Some I remembered, and some I did not, but I've now come to realize that none had been by chance or coincidence. Many were among the examples I've chosen to share with you in this book. Although I remembered thinking many of the people and opportunities were significant at the time, I didn't know why . . . until now.

As you prepare to think about your own chance encounters and coincidental opportunities, here are a couple of the examples I was shown by Christ, as they apply to some of the thirteen Elements of my Life.

A Faith-related chance encounter: *Relative to my faith, Lori Heredia had the most significant impact on the course of my life. Christ took me back to that October day in 2003 in, of all places, the recreation room of a senior citizens home. She was competing there in a Toastmasters speech contest and I met her when I went to cheer for one of her competitors. She is gentle, kind and caring and lives the most Christ-like life of anyone I have ever met. She never fails to walk the walk, and her light shone on me at a time when my Christian faith was waning. But today my faith remains solid because of the example she provided. Without a doubt, Faith is the core value most closely related to the impact she had on my life. Hope is the life driver I think of when Lori comes to mind, as she was a constant, overflowing source of it for me. The pastime we shared was public speaking, as we were both Toastmasters for many years. After the day we met, though, I cheered for her rather than her opponents!*

A Faith-related coincidental opportunity: *In 1980 I had an unexpected chance to go on a mission trip to the Amazon jungle in South America, arranged at the last minute when my classmates in my adult Sunday school class decided to raise the money to send me. Suddenly, there I was, living in the jungle again after all these years—literally back in the Stone Age—days from the nearest civilization (which was on the other side of the Andes Mountains). Through His eyes, I rediscovered the everlasting appreciation that experience taught me for the struggles that others in the world live with on a daily basis, struggles from which I was insulated by my* *middle class American upbringing. Most of my core values were reflected in this experience: Faith, for obvious reasons; Discovery, because my eyes were opened wide to a way of life that I barely knew existed; Independence, because the jungle is an isolated place that often demands that you be self-reliant in order to survive; Encouragement, because as a missionary I was there to be a source of support and reassurance to people who had never known that; and Influence, because we were there to inspire people through ideas they had never heard and didn't understand. We were there to share a vision of a more fulfilling life with the people, and to fulfill the vision we had for our own lives as well, so Vision was definitely the life driver at play here. Self-improvement has always been one of my passions, and it was a major reason I went to the jungle. I came back to America transformed and enriched, glad that I had taken a chance on people and geography that were unsettling because they were unknown to me.*

A Values-related coincidental opportunity: *In the summer of 1971, I had the honor of being chosen to attend Illinois Boys State in Springfield, though it was an honor I didn't seek and to this day I am unsure how it came about. Nevertheless, as I gazed through His eyes at my high-school self in an embarrassingly-tight Boys State t-shirt, I was sitting amid a mass of male humanity in a hot building at the Illinois State Fairgrounds attending leadership school. Boys State, run by the American Legion, was an experiment in the electoral process but it was something more. It was intended to instill the kind of values in high school kids that would make them model citizens down the road, and that goal hit the bulls-eye with me. I ran in my party's gubernatorial primary and for the first time was talking to other people about what I could—or would—do about things that mattered to them. My core value of Influence was getting an early test, experience that has served me well ever since, and it was here that I first began to notice that the decisions in my life were driven largely by Vision and Aspiration. And as you might guess, this exercise was fuel for one of my life's strongest passions, politics. It was all part of The Plan.*

A Health-related chance encounter: *Since 2006 I have had a blood disorder called ITP. Essentially, my immune system destroys my platelets and my blood won't clot. It has put me in the hospital numerous times and almost killed me once when I came close to bleeding out. Each year there is a conference where doctors and patients meet to discuss the latest breakthroughs in ITP research and treatment. Through His eyes, I returned to a hotel ballroom in Orlando and found myself back at the meeting that changed my life. For three years, I had avoided attending because the conference website made the event sound more like a sleep inducer than something transformational. Finally, in 2009, I decided to go because I had a feeling I needed to be there, and once again I had a front row seat as I discovered the reason why. The session was led by a doctor who had been researching the possible causes of ITP. For years no one was quite sure what caused it, but she was saying that her ongoing research now lead her to believe that one of the causes undoubtedly was mold. Upon arriving home I scoured every square inch of wall space in my home and ultimately moved a computer hutch that hadn't been away from the wall in five years. Behind it was a medicine ball sized patch of black mold that was so advanced the dry wall had begun to disintegrate and curl, revealing a very slow (and very small) plumbing leak in the wall that had been feeding the mold for a very long time. I sat two feet from that mold for years without knowing it was there. I had it remediated and then underwent months of chemo that forcibly shut down my immune system. Ultimately, thanks to a chance encounter with a doctor whose name I can't even remember, I have been in remission for four years. My Discovery core value sent me to the conference, Fear had been my decision driver and self-improvement was the passion that balanced that Fear. The Five Keys were at work protecting my health, preparing me for a new chapter in the journey to discover my Destiny.*

As you've just seen from reading about a couple of my Chance Encounters and Coincidental Opportunities, the significant people in your life aren't always people you end up knowing for years. Sometimes they're with you for just an hour or two and then are gone forever. In fact, some of them play such a fleeting (yet noteworthy) role in your life that you may remember them only by that role and not by name. Those with significant impact on the course of your life often are not lifelong friends of yours, nor is the specific role they play always significant in and of itself. Sometimes, their impact is simply to be a catalyst for the occurrence of future chance encounters or coincidental opportunities.

Just as the significant people in your life don't roll up in a limousine and walk the red carpet, your significant opportunities often don't announce themselves either. In fact, they may not seem all that significant at the time and often don't present themselves with earth-shattering fanfare. They're usually events or opportunities that don't linger in your life, transitory moments rather than lengthy, full-blown episodes. Like some chance encounters, they can sometimes simply provide a vehicle for the incidence of other chance encounters or coincidental opportunities.

Think now about the chance encounters and coincidental opportunities that have impacted the Elements of your life. You may find yourself doing a lot of thinking and it will no doubt overwhelm you, as it did me when I wrote this chapter. But as I wrote, I realized that the Third Key is the only one of the Five in which other people actively inject themselves into your search for your Personal Destiny. Opportunities and encounters will often happen *in spite* of you rather than *because* of actions you take. You have less control over what occurs in your life and, therefore, a greater responsibility to pay attention to what is happening around you and to take action to benefit from it. Because of this, the Third Key plays a significant role in your efforts to identify your earthbound Personal Destiny. Thinking about this may be difficult for you and it may take some time, but the payoff is worth it. Your Destiny will begin to come into focus when you complete The Third Key.

Reflect on each of the Elements of your life and try to think of one person in each Element with whom you had a chance encounter that impacted that particular part of your life in a significant way.

How did each person come into your life? In one sentence, how would you describe each of them? What specific impact did they each have on your life? On your values?

Continuing to reflect on the Elements of your life, try to think of a coincidental opportunity in each Element that dropped in front of you and impacted that particular part of your life in a significant way. How did each opportunity come about? How would you describe each one, in one sentence? What specific impact did each one have on your life, and on your values?

Again, thinking about these questions is important because the answers provide you with meaningful progress toward discovering your Personal Destiny. Write and tell me about a chance encounter or a coincidental opportunity that has made a difference in your life. I'd love to have you share it with me at JimMcComb@UndiscoveredHorizons.com.

8

Inspiration: The Fourth Key

What lies behind us and what lies before us are tiny matters compared to what lies within us.

Ralph Waldo Emerson (1803-1882)
Essayist, lecturer, poet

Now Christ took a Fourth Key, shaped like a lamp, and slipped it into the keyhole of the Fourth Great Door. As this door swung open, I saw myself seated amidst a small group of men and women in a hotel conference room in suburban Philadelphia in 1997. Through His eyes, I relived some of the most important days in my life . . . the days when I met—and got to know—my mentor. Those days had not come easily. It had been years since I had first been handed strategic planning responsibilities by an Oregon bank CEO because there was no one else on staff with the time to handle them. I took to planning like a duck takes to water, but always had this nagging feeling that I needed some formal guidance.

For several years I received direct mailers from someplace called the Centre for Strategic Management in San Diego, advertising strategic planning training offered in a multiple-day workshop setting. It was expensive and I was always hesitant to ask my employer for the money, thinking that this might not be the best educational option for me. I also was fearful I would discover that what I didn't know about planning would far exceed what I did know, meaning that I hadn't been doing the best possible job for my employer and now he would surely know it. So for several years I ignored both the mailings and those dogged feelings I had about needing formal guidance.

As the years went by, those notions became even more persistent. More and more often, they dominated my thoughts. They were pushy and insistent. Although I clearly remembered those days in Philadelphia, I had forgotten the nagging in my brain that led up to my decision to finally ask for the money and make a cross-country trip to learn from someone unknown to me except through the pages of a brochure. I didn't research the Centre in advance; I didn't do any due diligence; I didn't ask any questions or seek any references. Normally I would do all of those things, but in this case an inner voice was telling me to "Just go!"

Through His eyes I watched as I entered the meeting room for the opening night's session and extended my hand to three men who were already in the room. Two of them were consultants with the Centre and instructors for the workshop that would follow over the next couple of days. The third man, Steve Haines, was the CEO of the Centre and the lead instructor for the workshop. He was the guy I had read about in the brochure. The moment I grasped his hand, I knew he was someone special. Steve was a large man with a firm handshake and an overpowering presence. Yet he had a warmth about him that made me instantly comfortable. As I settled in for that opening evening session and relived the scene through Christ, I was beginning to sense what I now know full well today: the next few days would be some of the most important of my lifetime.

As it turned out, there was a lot more to strategic planning than I knew but in just a couple of days Steve bridged that knowledge gap for me. I liked him, I respected him, I soaked up every word he had to say and I connected with him. He became my mentor during our days together in that conference room, although neither of us knew it at the time. Steve saw something in me that I was only just beginning to see in myself: a gift for strategic thinking and management. A few short months after that workshop, I was a partner in the Centre and was running their Denver office. In less than a year I had morphed from a self-taught rookie to a key leadership role in the largest strategic planning consultancy in the world.

Since the time you and I were children, we've often been preoccupied with thoughts that pop into our heads over and over and over. They're persistent and tenacious notions that sometimes lead us by the hand down a path toward specific actions, conclusions or decisions. Sometimes they simply plant ideas or concepts or beliefs or feelings in our brains and hearts and expect us to figure out where to go from there. Rather than leading us by the hand, persistent notions just shine a light on the path and point into the distance.

Whether they lead us by the hand or not, it's difficult to ignore these recurring thoughts although we often don't act on them for one reason or another. Perhaps we view them as too time consuming, or too expensive, or contrary to our core values (even though we may be unsure specifically what those values are). Sometimes we don't understand what those thoughts are saying and other times, because they seem uninteresting, we simply don't care what they're trying to tell us.

My thoughts clearly led me to make the decision to go Philadelphia and to take advantage of the opportunities that awaited me there. The ideas that stalked me in the years before I wrote this book were more obscure. They pointed to a path, but I was unable to see it clearly because I didn't read the signals properly. I thought about Destiny constantly, but wasn't sure why. I understood that I had been born with a purpose, but was still a bit fuzzy on that purpose and didn't realize that it had such a specific connection to other people. I had a hazy idea for a book, and wrote down my thoughts every now and then, but I wasn't sure what the intended result was to be. After six years of enduring my false starts on this book, six years of planting constant thoughts in my mind that I couldn't put into any semblance of order and six years of listening to me talk about Destiny and not do anything about it, God finally grew tired of trying to get through to me. Ultimately, it took death on an operating table and an extraordinary journey to a place few living people ever see in order for me to get the message. God had to be more direct with me. The Day I Went To Heaven, I finally "got it."

Even though few of us are ever summoned to Heaven—and sent back—during our lifetime, we all have persistent notions. They come to us in a variety of forms. Some people claim to hear actual voices. Although the rest of us might wonder about the long-term mental stability of those people, I did actually see proof during my visit to Heaven that the Lord can occasionally come to us in a voice that we interpret to be audible. Others of us daydream and are viewed by the rest of the population as lazy or as children in adult suits who are lost in fantasy and simply never grow up. Often, though, daydreams are a manifestation of our Personal Destiny, a way for God to paint a picture for us of the role He has prepared us to fulfill. Throughout history, most inventors and artists and leading-edge thinkers have spent significant time in daydreams, envisioning the various possibilities for the ideas they will ultimately bring to life.

Virtually all of us live a lifetime filled with what we call intuition. Women usually get the credit for having a perfected sense of intuition, although all of us are capable of being intuitive. Intuition is with you every time you suspect that something might be true, every time your instincts push you in a certain direction, every time you have insight into a particular issue or problem. If you have a "hunch" or a "gut feeling," your intuition is working. You've certainly heard that "perception is reality" and often perception is also intuition. Your conscience is a particular intuition that often steers you back to your core values (even if you are not consciously aware of what they are) and shines a light on the difference between right and wrong.

Regardless of the form in which you may receive nagging thoughts, you definitely have these persistent notions, and you have them for a reason. They are God's way of speaking to you and if they're interpreted correctly, and acted upon appropriately and promptly, they serve as clues to your earthbound Personal Destiny. They are The Fourth Key to discovering your Horizon . . . The Key of Inspiration.

Persistent notions are with you from the day you're born, although you don't become conscious of them until you're old enough to think for yourself. Then several years go by before you begin to think more deeply about them and to question what they might mean. Most of us live a significant portion of our lives before we learn how to interpret the meaning of these thoughts that keep appearing on our radar screen, and how to determine which of them are destined to play a role in our future. In some cases we never learn to interpret their meaning, resulting in untold lost opportunities to discover, and fulfill, our Personal Destiny.

You might wonder at this point how to tell the difference between a persistent notion and a daydream, since daydreams (such as my quest for the White House) can be persistent too and can come to us many times over the course of a lifetime. The difference is that daydreams are often impractical fantasies that don't inspire you to take any specific action, or, given the nature of some daydreams, make it impossible for you to take action. Therefore, daydreams are often difficult to accomplish and are rarely ever realized. They generally grow out of something you hear or see or experience in your day-to-day existence that cultivates a desire in you to live a life that you perceive to be better than the one you have now. You might dream of winning the lottery, of being retired, of living on the beach on a tropical island, of being the CEO of the organization for which you work, or any one of a thousand different things (including being President of the United States).

There are instances when daydreams inspire action and are not impractical fantasies. Those would be the daydreams of the inventors and artists and thought leaders that I mentioned earlier. Although even their daydreams can dissipate without results just as ours usually do, there is something different about their daydreams. They have a greater chance for fulfillment because they generally grow out of something the dreamer hears or sees or experiences that cultivates a desire in them to improve the lives of others. Service to others is the difference and once that benevolent end enters the equation, most daydreams of this type morph into persistent notions until they are fulfilled.

Persistent notions, on the other hand, are sudden, yet sustained, instincts and urges that are generally about things that come out of the blue and are not related to—or prompted by—anything you have previously seen or heard or experienced. As I've told you, I was bombarded by thoughts of Destiny and life purpose for six years before The Day I Went to Heaven. I had no idea where they came from. I had never read any articles about Destiny, or heard any motivational speaker talk about it, or watched any movies or television shows that dealt with Destiny as a theme. One day, all of a sudden, the thoughts were there and they stayed there, stubbornly demanding action. I don't remember that day, or the day I finally realized that thoughts of Destiny had commandeered my mind for a significant portion of every single day.

Dreams will generally yield to new dreams once common sense or reality eventually get through to our sub-conscience and convince us that we probably will never win the lottery or live in Tahiti or be president. Persistent notions, if they're the real thing, don't yield until you finally get the message and act on them, or until God grabs you by the shoulder and spins you around and forces you to act on them. I've always been a stubborn person who was determined to go my own way, in my own time (remember that Independence is one of my core values), but I'm convinced to this day that my appearance in Heaven occurred because God had run out of patience waiting for me to discover—and act on—my Destiny.

Persistent notions can show up in any of the thirteen Elements of Life, but probably not in all of them because, as Christ showed me, genuine persistent notions only occur a few times in a lifetime. Through His eyes, I was reminded of four that occurred in mine.

I saw myself as a young grade school student seated at a long table in the basement of the Third Presbyterian Church in Rockford, Illinois. It was summer in the early 1960's and I was in the midst of twenty children gathered around that table, making stand-up crosses out of little blocks of wood and staining them. My cross found a place atop my parents' console television for nearly a decade. Now, more than fifty years later, it still exists and sits on my nightstand next to one of my wedding pictures. The point of this fleeting event in my life was not the cross, but what I was thinking as I made it.

Since I was just a child, I had no recollection of what I was thinking that day. Now, though, it was as if I was reading my own mind. As I fashioned that little icon, I realized for the first time in my young life that it stood for something. The Son of God had been on that cross. God. If His Son was real, then He had to be real. He had created everything around me. That persistent notion planted a seed that day that eventually grew into my Christian faith.

I witnessed that faith come full circle as the scene shifted to Cal Tech in Pasadena, California. It was a scene still fresh in my mind, as it occurred in the fall of 2006. I was in a lecture hall at a meeting of the Skeptics Society, a group of scientists, professors, engineers and other learned professionals who had come to hear Sam Harris, one of America's most prominent atheist authors. Of the two or three hundred in the room that day, all were atheists except the six of us who were bold enough to raise our hands when the chair asked if there were any Christians present.

Then he asked if any of us would like to say anything. I was the only one who stood, and normally I wouldn't have challenged a group like this in their meeting. But thoughts of that cross suddenly popped into my head—a persistent notion that had been with me for years—and my belief in God spilled out as if a dam had just burst. I told them that I believed everything happened for a reason, and that we had each been created by God for a specific reason.

So, if everything happens for a reason and Life is indeed not some random, coincidental accident, then our brains weren't created by some big bang. They were deliberately designed and created by someone, for some specific reason. Things that complex *that actually work are designed in a systematic way, by something or someone. They don't just happen. They are created. I asked them to think about the greatest inventions of our history. The telephone, the computer, miracle drugs, the wheel, television, the automobile, the light bulb, the camera. None was the by-product of an explosion. Explosions destroy. Hands and minds create, and all of these great inventions were created by the hand and mind of someone. And when great ideas become great products and processes, there is always a purpose. Greatness is never created "just because" someone was bored that day and had nothing better to do. There is always a purpose . . . to make life faster, simpler, happier, safer, more efficient, less expensive or more entertaining. Those are also the reasons God made us. The jeers began almost immediately and I convinced no one that I was right, yet that one speech finally brought a notion full-circle that had been persistent in me for more than four decades. Faith was clearly established as one my core values, driven by Hope and sustained by the passion for public speaking that God had given me*

Through His eyes, I returned to my childhood and was looking down at myself, staring into my own eyes. I had wandered a couple of blocks from my house on Fremont Street in Janesville, Wisconsin that fall day in 1959. I lay on my back in an open field near Craig High School and stared up at the drifting cloud formations. As my five-year-old imagination saw faces passing by in those clouds I thought about what my kindergarten teacher, Miss Kinz, had said in school earlier that day. "You're all here with something special to do," she had said. "Your life has a purpose. You just need to find out what it is."

As I looked up into the clouds, certain that I was staring into the face of God Himself, I wondered what my "something special" would be. That question became a persistent notion that stuck with me for fifty-two years, until The Day I Went to Heaven. As a result, Discovery developed into one of my core values, driven by my Aspiration to find purpose (and by my Fear of possibly discovering that I had no purpose) and sustained by my passion for writing. This book is the evidence.

We've all heard that phrase "love at first sight" and generally associate it with physical attraction or with the feeling that you've known someone for your entire life even though you just met them. The day I met my wife Sally I definitely felt each of those things as I fell in love at first sight, yet I felt something else as well. I had this sense that the two of us were destined to be together, that we were intended not only to live and love together but to be a team that would accomplish something specific together. It was a persistent notion that pursued me almost daily for the first two years we were together, although I had no clue what that "something special" would be.

I didn't tell Sally that this feeling was stalking me and only just a few months ago learned that her intuition was leading her to the same conclusion. Unbeknownst to either of us, we spent about a year on a joint search for that "something special." We went to a Millionaire Mind seminar for two days and to a Stores Online meeting, searching for something we could do together toward the realization of our separate versions of "something special." Our search ended The Day I Went to Heaven.

Almost from the very second that I woke up in the hospital, I realized that Sally was in my life to help me realize my Personal Destiny and that I was in her life to play the same role for her. We had been brought together for a reason, because our Destinies were complementary and because we each had uniquely innate skills and abilities that would be of help to the other in their pursuit of both the Undiscovered Horizon and the Ultimate Destination. We were, in essence, teammates who were headed in the same direction. I now understand that this is what it means to be soul mates. If you meet and marry the person whom God has intended for you, then the love and honor and respect that you share are actually ingredients in the fulfillment of your own Personal Destiny.

Strange as it may seem, my core value of Independence was at work here. Driven by the Dreams that Sally and I share, this persistent notion showed me that none of us is truly independent. We all need help in order to play the role we're intended to play in Life, not only from our soul mate, but from our network of friends and colleagues as well. That explains my passion for social networking!

Can you recall those persistent notions that have relentlessly pursued you over the years? Perhaps you've acted on them and put them to rest; maybe they're still on your mind as you read this. Remember, though, that we're not talking about thoughts that simply remind you to perform a specific act such as going to the store or picking up your daughter from soccer practice or finishing a particular report for work tomorrow. Persistent notions are thoughts that cannot be addressed with a single, simple action. Thoughts that potentially have a strategic impact on your life and yet often don't even lead to a specific action.

For example, a year ago you may have informally counseled a friend at work who was having difficulty with the boss. She successfully navigated the pain and the stress with your help and thanked you as she embarked on the remainder of her life with a renewed sense of self-worth. Since your visits with her concluded you've continued to think about the way you felt when your words resulted in a happy ending for her, about the way she felt as she talked to you and about the fulfillment that washed over you as you helped to make life better for someone else. Eventually you yield to the thoughts and go back to school to seek a degree in counseling so that you can pursue a career in which you help people like your friend from work every day.

Or perhaps you see a feature story about a poor country in Africa on the nightly news and are haunted for months or years by visions of children without homes or access to education or enough food to eat. Eventually you yield to those thoughts as well and sign up for service with a charitable organization. You relocate to Africa, where you help drill wells for clean water and teach the people effective farming methods or basic medical care techniques. Perhaps you're a health care professional who travels there to provide medical or dental services at no cost, or a retired business professional who teaches the people how to start and run their own small businesses.

Occasionally persistent notions hit a bit closer to home. If you can't have children, as was the case for Cindy and I, thoughts of the joys you're missing come to you every time you see happy families at a pizza parlor or at a youth soccer game or in church when the babies are dedicated. It's painful until you realize that you can adopt a child who needs a family and you take action, as Cindy and I did.

Perhaps you drive past the local rescue mission every day for years as you commute to work. The mission drifts in and out of your thoughts until you decide one day to send them a check. Then you become a volunteer, serving holiday meals, and eventually take a seat on their board of directors. While a board member, you negotiate a relationship between the mission and your employer that results in work opportunities for some of those who live temporarily at the mission.

Consider each of the thirteen Elements of your life. What were those thoughts that were with you for a long time before you acted, or those thoughts that you actively resisted? What thoughts continue to preoccupy you, even today? You probably won't think of more than three or four persistent notions that were profound enough, or tenacious enough, to be life-changers for you, but you *will* think of them. If they were stubborn enough you will still recall those notions easily, particularly if you have yet to take action on some of them.

How did each thought on which you've already acted specifically impact the course of your life? If there is a thought or two that continue to nag you, demanding action, how will taking that action affect your life? How did your persistent notions initially come to mind? How might they be clues to your Personal Destiny?

Although pondering these questions may seem a bit challenging, remember that the Fourth Key brings you within the shadow of the mountains on your Horizon. One more Key and you'll be ready to put it all together. Before moving on, though, remember to share your persistent notions with me!

9

Inherence: The Fifth Key

God has given you a gift from His great variety of spiritual gifts. Use them well to serve one another.

Saint Peter the Apostle (1 A.D.-64 A.D.)
1 Peter 4:10 (NLT)

As Christ produced the final key, in the shape of The Cross, He told me that it, of the five keys he had shown me, was the most important of all. As the Fifth Great Door swung open, through His eyes I saw that this most important key to discovering Personal Destiny was actually something that He had shown me earlier: the Intrinsic Gift that is already inherent in you on the day you're born.

Each of the keys used to gain access to the five Great Doors has special significance. The arrow symbolizes the Direction that the First Key provides to our lives through core values and life drivers that define our choices and decisions in life, while the book is representative of the knowledge that we acquire through the Second Key, Unconscious Attraction. An unknown face on the Third Key signifies the chance encounters and coincidences that shape Opportunity in our life, and the light of the lamp provides the Inspiration of the Fourth Key. The Cross is the symbol of God's greatest gift to humankind, Eternal Life, and so it seemed to be an appropriate choice to represent the Inherence of the Fifth Key, God's intrinsic earthbound gift to us.

Once again, through His eyes, I found myself revisiting a part of my childhood that had long ago disappeared from my radar screen. It was the summer of 1965 and I was hot stuff because I was heading into sixth grade and would be one of the "big kids." The Park District in Rockford had an active summer camp program and my parents always sent my brother and sister and me each summer. Nature Jaunt and Tall Pines were day camps and they were for the younger elementary school kids. But as a sixth grader, I had arrived. I was in the Wilderness Camp, which meant an entire week away from home, south of the city, sleeping under the stars in rural Atwood Park.

Speaking of stars, along with all of the standard camp fare like arts & crafts, canoeing, archery and outdoor cooking, we got to study the stars one night. Although my memories of that summer no longer exist, I now had the opportunity to look on as my group of campers studied astronomy one evening before breaking out the sleeping bags. Our group counselor had a telescope that we took turns using to scan the heavens, but it was a search that the group did with the naked eye that caught my attention as I watched that evening unfold before me once again.

The counselor pointed out the North Star and said that travelers used that star for guidance on long journeys in the days before modern inventions came along to help people find their way. The North Star was a good directional star because it hardly ever seems to move and because it's brighter than most of the other stars in the sky. It was easy for all of the kids to spot, and from there we were able to see, with a bit more difficulty, the other stars that combine with the North Star to form the Little Dipper constellation.

I was curious what this particular scene had to do with my Destiny. Through Christ's eyes, I saw the Little Dipper up close and learned that this constellation (and certainly others as well) illustrates the role of the Fifth Key in our lives. God placed the North Star in the skies as an anchor and a reliable constant upon which travelers depended to reach their destination. Similarly, he has endowed us each with an Intrinsic Gift at birth that serves as our anchor and reliable constant as we pursue the fulfillment of our earthbound Personal Destiny.

Our Intrinsic Gift is an innate talent we're born with that is the very core of what makes us unique among all of the billions of people who inhabit earth today. Just as the North Star is the central focus of the Little Dipper, our Intrinsic Gift—once we're aware of it and use it properly and effectively—becomes the focus of our existence. Just as the North Star needs other stars in order to form a constellation, our Intrinsic Gift needs a supporting group of skills, abilities and talents in order to endow us with the capability to fulfill our Personal Destiny.

Together, your core Intrinsic Gift and all of the skills, abilities and talents that surround it are a package that uniquely equips you to successfully pursue your life's purpose. The package is unique because no one else has been endowed by God with that exact same combination of skills, abilities, talents and gifts, to the same degree in which you received them. We all have been uniquely prepared by God to accomplish something specific for Him while we're on earth.

Your Intrinsic Gift is the fully-developed core talent that was inherent in you on the day you were born. You never had to go to school to learn it, or hire a coach to help you develop it or ask anyone to show you how to do it. You have natural, instinctive ability in this area and others consistently see this talent in you and compliment you on your ability. You are confident of your expertise, in spite of the fact that you have never had any formal education or training in the area that is your core Intrinsic Gift. You were aware that it is the foundation of your earthbound Personal Destiny, even before you knew you had a Destiny.

The North Star Identified

My Intrinsic Gift was the one thing that Christ didn't reveal to me in Heaven directly because He said I already knew what it was, since many people in my lifetime have already identified it for me. At first I was puzzled, until I thought about it for a moment and realized that He was right. Throughout my entire life, family, friends, co-workers and colleagues have told me numerous times that I was good at counseling, guiding, encouraging and advising both people and organizations. I've helped co-workers plan their career paths, coached organizational leaders wanting to hone their skills, assisted people with strategic life planning, facilitated the definition and execution of strategic plans for numerous business organizations and aided friends who needed help properly assessing problems in their lives and deciding what to do about them. You have seen evidence of my Intrinsic Gift through the many accounts I've shared with you in this book. You've looked, right alongside me, through His eyes as I've been shown both the origin of my Destiny and my capacity to fulfill it. Those of you who know me personally have most likely also witnessed my Gift in action in some direct way at least once or twice over the years. I have probably seen yours as well.

I have never had formal educational training in strategic planning, coaching, career planning, life planning or counseling, yet people and organizations seek me out to perform those services because I come highly recommended and I help people get results. I'm *good* at those things and always have been, yet I never formally learned how to do them. I just *knew* how to do them. He was right. I already knew what my Intrinsic Gift was, and have known for many years. I just never connected my inherent abilities with anything called Destiny.

You're already aware of your Intrinsic Gift as well. Like I have, you've heard many of those who know you well compliment you on something you're *very good* at doing, and they all seem to mention the same thing. You think about it for a moment every time someone observes your larger-than-life talent and you realize that, in fact, you *are* good at it. In fact, you're *very good* at it and that surprises you because you never took a class to learn it or hired a coach to help you perfect it. You're already an expert and, until now, you've never been quite sure why. As you complete the Fifth Key, the time has come to identify—and fully recognize—your core Intrinsic Gift. Thoughtfully consider the questions in the next two paragraphs.

What are you "good at," according to *others*? What skill, ability or talent have friends, family, co-workers, relatives, mentors, employers and others most often recognized in you as inherent genius? In order to be your core Intrinsic Gift, it needs to be something that you do exceedingly well but were never taught or shown how to do. What skill, ability or talent have *you* noticed in yourself that you've been inherently "good at" since you were a young child? When you've most enjoyed helping others, what is it that you've usually been doing? What one thing in your life so far has most energized, exhilarated and inspired you? What spiritual legacy do you want to leave behind, and why is that particular legacy important to you?

Is the skill, ability or talent that *you* believe to be your Intrinsic Gift consistent with the observations your family, friends and colleagues have made over the years? Do *they* recognize the same Intrinsic Gift in you that you see? If not, to what do you attribute the differences? Does any resemblance exist between their conclusion and yours? Could your Gift actually be that similarity?

As you reflect on your answers to the questions in the previous two paragraphs, note the common theme that is certain to surface. That is your Intrinsic Gift. Think about the thirteen Elements of your Life; in what ways is your Gift at work in each of them? The answer points directly to your Destiny.

The Rest of the Little Dipper

Just as the North Star cannot form the Little Dipper all by itself, your core Intrinsic Gift alone cannot deliver the full range of skill, ability and talent that you need to fulfill your earthbound Personal

Destiny. Support is needed from a group of secondary intrinsic gifts that were also inherent in you on the day you were born, although not as completely developed as your core Gift.

You develop your secondary intrinsic gifts throughout the course of your lifetime through formal education, informal study, coaching and mentoring from others. Generally, you're comfortable with your expertise in these areas, though not as boldly confident as you are in your core Intrinsic Gift capabilities. On occasion others have observed, and complimented, your proficiency or expertise in some of these secondary areas. As is true of your core Gift, you have natural, instinctive ability in these areas, however, unlike your core Gift, these secondary intrinsic gifts are not necessarily reflected throughout all thirteen of the Elements of your Life. They do, however, support your core Gift and are a part of the foundation upon which your earthbound Personal Destiny is built.

When God created you and me, He also created an endless number of skills, abilities and talents with which to endow us. Acting, networking, encouraging, goal-setting, budgeting, leading, repairing and imagining are just a few of the competencies in which you might have aptitude, proficiency or expertise. The Resource section of the *Undiscovered Horizons Personal Destiny Plan* workbook lists nearly one hundred skills and talents, divided into eight major categories. By no means an exhaustive inventory, it is intended simply to stimulate your thinking as you ponder the questions in the paragraph below.

In addition to your core Intrinsic Gift, what else are you "good at," according to *others*? In which additional skill, ability and talent areas have friends, family, co-workers, relatives, mentors, employers and others recognized your inherent genius at least once during your lifetime? Which skills, abilities and talents have *you* noticed in yourself that you're inherently "good at," although you've needed a little education, training or coaching to become as skilled in those areas as you are? Which of the skills, abilities and talents that you (and others) have noticed are effective complements to your core Intrinsic Gift and fit comfortably with it?

Are the skills, abilities and talents that *you* believe to be your secondary intrinsic gifts consistent with the observations your family, friends and colleagues have made over the years? Do *they* recognize any of the same secondary gifts that you see? If not, to what do you attribute the differences? Does any commonality exist between their conclusions and yours?

As you reflect on your answers to the questions in the previous two paragraphs, look for the gifts that are most often recognized in you by others, as well as those gifts that are identified by you *and* by others. Those are your secondary intrinsic gifts. In what ways are those gifts at work in the thirteen Elements of your Life? The answer points directly to your Destiny.

You now have the Five Keys in hand and are at the base of the mountains. You're literally at the Horizon. You've finally arrived.

10

Horizon: Discovered

*You have not lived today until you've done something
for someone who can never repay you.*

John Bunyan (1628-1688)
Writer, preacher, author of *The Pilgrim's Progress*

When I was young I always wondered who I would grow up to be. Since we were in the early days of space travel, most of the kids I knew wanted to be astronauts. The Gemini astronauts were our heroes, and the idea of going into space, while scary to a six-year-old, nevertheless held a certain adventurous attraction. We had other heroes too. President Kennedy, Mickey Mantle and Sandy Koufax, and just about every cowboy star on TV. Yet even at the age of six, I knew that I would probably never fly in space or play major league baseball. But what kind of a contribution *would* I make?

I continued to wonder what purpose my life would serve until I was well into my fifties, when I began to get a glimpse of it about five or six years before The Day I Went To Heaven. As a corporate strategic planner for many years, I decided one day to begin teaching the principles of strategic planning to people so that they could live more successful and fulfilling personal lives. I put together a workshop and advertised it as "Two Hours That Will Change Your Life" because I believed that strategic planning provides the focus, clarity and sense of direction that people need to lead successful lives. Hundreds of people signed up for the class over the years and the evaluations were always good.

Those evaluations were the yardstick that I had intended to use to measure my own success at delivering meaningful material. That changed the day I went to the mailbox and found the first in a constant stream of thank-you cards, letters and emails that came to me over the next few years. Those who had participated in the class were writing to tell me about new careers, new degrees, new families and new lives that had resulted from investing two hours in learning how to strategically plan their future. One note said, "You were right. That class did turn out to be two hours that changed my life." A thank-you card said, "Thank you very much for teaching me how to figure out what I wanted in life, and how to go after it." Another note said, "I wish you'd offered this class years ago" and still another said, "The ideas you shared got me to thinking . . . and that was a game-changer for me."

As the cards and letters came, they gave me a psychological lift unlike anything I had ever experienced before. Helping people had always given me a measure of great satisfaction, but this was different. About more than just serving people, this class had unexpectedly become a vehicle for *transforming* people, those who could never repay me. The class, you see, had been offered at no charge.

Stations of Destiny

And so, I had begun to find fulfillment through, of all things, a class I had designed on the spur of the moment and had decided, for no particular reason, to offer to people free of charge.

Although I wasn't making money, I was getting far more valuable compensation—helping people through one-on-one contact, thinking strategically and delivering encouragement, inspiration and transformation—both to those in the class, and to myself. Was this my Horizon? The Father had hinted at it earlier as I knelt in awe at the foot of His Throne. Now, through Christ's eyes, I was about to arrive at my Horizon at long last.

Suddenly the walls and windows that had admitted only rays of dazzling light into the room seemed to dissolve and I found myself completely bathed in those rays, standing on a hill above a river of bright, vibrant color unlike any that I had seen before. Across the river were twenty-four hills overgrown with lush green and yellow vegetation, and atop each of the hills stood a young child. Although each wore a flowing white robe, and it was not possible for me to discern their facial features or skin color, I instinctively knew that there were twelve boys and twelve girls. Each held a ring containing five keys in their hands.

Through His eyes, I learned that each of the hills represented a Station of Destiny, and that each child was actually a soul about to be born with an earthbound Personal Destiny that related to the Station upon which they were standing. The keys were the Five Keys that He had shown me earlier . . . the Five Keys that lead all of us to the discovery of our own individual Horizon. The lush vegetation represented the spiritual food that nourishes us during our lifetime as we pursue the fulfillment of our own unique Personal Destiny.

One by one, in no particular order, He introduced them to me, cautioning that their Station was not the occupation they would hold someday, but rather their "station" in Life . . . the role and responsibility that He had chosen, and uniquely prepared, each of them to fulfill.

Because this role and responsibility is about purpose, it is necessarily much bigger than any job. He showed me that jobs limit us to a specific set of duties and tasks and accountabilities, and provide few opportunities for us to truly use our intrinsic gifts to give other people what they actually need from us. Each Station is an overarching role that permeates every one of the thirteen Elements of Life. Your Station is reflected in your marriage, your career, your volunteer and leisure activities and your home life. It is reflected in the way you manage your health and your finances, and in the way you parent your children and interact with friends, co-workers and family.

He presented each Station as a compendium of many related roles. Each soul born to a particular Station would fulfill one or more of those roles in Life. These are the twenty-five Stations of Destiny that were introduced to me.

The Clarifier resolves situations, solves problems and mysteries, explains, interprets and clarifies difficult concepts, fixes things, reunites hearts, answers questions, exposes untruths, unscrambles code, and settles arguments.

The Teacher imparts wisdom and skills, communicates concepts, information and techniques, demonstrates correctness, explains complex issues and concepts, instills a joy of learning in everyone they touch, equips others for success, informs the uninformed and introduces new ideas.

The Architect designs procedures and lifestyles, builds cultures and roads and companies, invents products and approaches, generates ideas, engineers processes, drives change and brings art and music and dance to life.

The Healer reconciles emotions, rebuilds self-esteem and character, restores physical, mental, emotional and spiritual health, cures diseases of the mind, body and heart, mends broken spirits and tends to the needs of the neglected.

The Nurturer cares for those unable to care for themselves, encourages those unable to hope for themselves, cultivates growth and provides direction in those too young to make decisions for themselves and fosters and adopts those with nowhere to turn.

The Entertainer amuses, diverts and delights, and performs so that others will laugh and cry and think and learn and relax.

The Catalyst *makes things happen, enables other things to happen, brings people together, mediates disputes, brokers deals, initiates new ideas, organizes life and drives results.*

The Pioneer *takes risks others avoid, discovers things no one else ever sees, embarks on voyages to destinations others avoid, seeks adventure—even when it's hard to find—and incubates new ideas.*

The Guardian *rescues those in trouble, guards against mayhem, ensures the safety and quality of Life, watches over valuables and defends the defenseless.*

The Administrator *manages and supervises the daily operations of Life in the home and the office, is often the proprietor of business ventures and brings order and direction to processes and programs.*

The Host *facilitates social interaction, meets the needs of others, gets energized when entertaining others and is the master of ceremonies of Life.*

The Leader *drives results, inspires others, creates vision, drives action and change, is a source of direction for projects, organizations and initiatives, displays self-directed initiative and is the architect of success.*

The Organizer *synchronizes and harmonizes Life, develops systems and processes and categories, brings order and structure to projects, initiatives and organizations, plans and prepares, and initiates action whenever and wherever it is needed.*

The Scholar *conducts research, develops new lines of thought, becomes immersed in specific topics and issues, consistently hones their intellect and exists to acquire knowledge and to share it with others.*

The Interpreter *translates knowledge or data for others, analyzes and explains complex issues and problems, provides commentary on the issues of the day and might be multi-lingual.*

The Ally *champions causes, initiatives and ideas, provides assistance to others whenever or wherever it is needed and often follows rather than leading.*

The Motivator *skillfully communicates the oral and written word, inspires those with whom they communicate and is a primary source of influence in driving the action necessary to make Life happen.*

The Regulator *follows the rules and insists that others do as well, carries out orders, insists on compliance with the law, frequently imposes their will on others and administers the order that keeps society functioning.*

The Reporter *updates others on a regular basis, advises superiors, issues reports, enlightens others about things of which they were not aware, communicates through printed, broadcast and digital media and shares information with the authorities about the activities of others.*

The Judge *critiques the performance of people and processes and products, appraises the value of things and ideas and people, weighs the importance of choices and alternatives and determines outcomes after assessing the facts.*

The Steward *keeps the books and records, watches over property and people and is the custodian of all things valuable and important.*

The Advocate *promotes organizations, companies, causes, ideas, products, and people, upholds values, stimulates change and creates awareness.*

The Solicitor *identifies and recruits resources that meet the needs of organizations and people, drafts people for unpleasant assignments and engages others in activities that contribute to their personal and professional growth.*

The Patron *invests their own time, money, ideas and personal energy to ensure that initiatives, causes, companies and organizations that are important have the opportunity to exist and succeed, and empowers them to reach their greatest possible level of potential.*

After I was introduced to each child they faded from my view, as did the hill upon which each was standing. As the last hill vanished, I noticed that there was no horizon beyond it. In fact, there was now *a vast expanse of nothingness where the hills and the children had once been. Only the river of color remained before me.*

*I was standing on the only remaining hill, and for the first time noticed that there was lush green and yellow vegetation under my feet and a ring of five keys in my hand . . . identical to the one Christ had held earlier as He unlocked the five Great Doors. He had told me that there were twenty-five Stations of Destiny, yet had introduced me to only twenty-four. The remaining Station—***The Pathfinder***—was mine. As a Pathfinder, I consult with those who seek a better way, coach those with talent to develop, mentor those with potential and promise, counsel those who need guidance and direction and guide those who have lost their way.*

I learned that the river of color was not actually a river at all, but rather a passageway through which the children . . . the new souls . . . had passed to begin living their various Stations, armed with the Five Keys. What I had seen as a river, He called the Fabric of Life.

The Fabric of Life

The common threads that are inherent in each of your Five Keys, when woven together, create your Fabric of Life. That Fabric, of course, is actually your Destiny and fully understanding the threads that comprise it will help you identify which of the twenty-five Stations of Destiny is yours. Understanding those common threads comes as a result of taking a thorough look at each of your Five Keys:

Core Values & Life Drivers. What do your core values have in common? In what ways do they seem alike? How have they collectively influenced or shaped your life? What recurring theme runs through the paragraph you wrote about yourself based on those values? Which of your life drivers appears to be the catalyst for most of your life decisions? Why?

Passions & Pastimes. What do your passions and pastimes have in common? What recurring theme seems to be inherent in all of them? In what similar way did you acquire most of your passions and pastimes? In what similar ways have each of them influenced or shaped your life?

Chance Encounters & Coincidental Opportunities. What do the significant people with whom you've had chance encounters have in common? What attributes do they share? In what similar ways have they influenced or shaped your life? In what similar way did you meet most of your chance encounters? What do your most significant coincidental opportunities have in common? What recurring theme runs through all of them? In what similar ways have they influenced or shaped your life? In what related way did you experience most of your coincidental opportunities?

Persistent Notions. What do your recurring thoughts have in common? What repetitive theme seems to run through all, or most, of them? In what similar ways have they influenced or shaped your life? Under what similar circumstances do most of your recurring thoughts seem to come to you?

Core and Secondary Intrinsic Gifts. What do your core and secondary gifts have in common? What recurring theme seems to be a part of all of them? In what similar ways have they influenced and shaped your life? In what similar ways, and for what similar ends, do you use your gifts?

Finding & Fulfilling Your Destiny: Step Five

The **fifth step in finding and fulfilling your own unique Personal Destiny** is identifying the common threads and synergies that exist in your core values, passions and pastimes, chance encounters and coincidental opportunities, persistent notions and intrinsic gifts. Once these common threads and synergies are identified, you can more clearly understand their impact on the thirteen Elements of your Life and your Station of Destiny becomes easy to identify.

The common threads or themes that are inherent in each of your Five Keys should all point toward one Station of Destiny and that Station will generally be the answer to each of the questions below.

In rare instances, one or two of the answers may point toward a different, although somewhat related, Station.

- Which Station of Destiny is most consistent with the common theme inherent in your core values and life drivers?
- Which Station of Destiny is most consistent with the common theme inherent in your passions and pastimes?
- Which Station of Destiny is most consistent with the common theme inherent in your chance encounters and coincidental opportunities?
- Which Station of Destiny is most consistent with the common theme inherent in your persistent notions?
- Which Station of Destiny is most consistent with the common theme inherent in your core and secondary intrinsic gifts?

Congratulations! You've identified your Station of Destiny! You're about to learn how to make that Destiny unique and personal to you, and once you know that your Horizon will no longer be Undiscovered! In the meantime, I'd love to know which Station of Destiny is yours. Please take a moment to share it with me at JimMcComb@UndiscoveredHorizons.com.

The river . . . the Fabric . . . changed course and began to flow into the nothingness that was left behind when the souls had departed and the hills had disappeared. I realized that I had initially seen nothing there because I had discovered my Horizon. As He revealed my Station of Destiny, I found that I had finally arrived at my Horizon and was now looking toward what lay beyond it. I knew that the Ultimate Destination—fulfillment of my earthbound Personal Destiny—was out there but I couldn't see it because the ending to my Life story has yet to be written. God has provided my Destiny, but its fulfillment remains up to me.

As the hill began to disappear beneath my feet I sensed that it would soon be time for me to leave Heaven and the wonders that I had seen through His eyes. I drew closer to the flowing Fabric that would return me to Life to resume my own Incredible Odyssey, the journey toward fulfillment of the Station of Destiny that He had designed for me.

Before I could leave, He had one final wonder to reveal . . . the power within each of us that makes our Stations of Destiny so unique, and so very Personal.

11

The Power in You

Let us remember that the greatest earthly gifts we can provide are our presence and influence while we live, and a magnificent memory of our life once we're gone.

Chuck Swindoll (1934-present)
Pastor, author, educator

In December of 2012 I was the keynote speaker at a destiny-themed event put on by a leadership mentoring organization for business and professional women called Business Women Rising. The group's leader had heard about this book and asked me to share my story, which would be the first time I had ever discussed *Undiscovered Horizons* in public.

I was invited to speak at the event six months before it actually took place and, because I wanted everything to be right, I took the entire six months to prepare for that "first time." Astonishingly, it was not until the night before the presentation that the real meaning of what I had to share actually became clear to me. This wasn't to be a story about Jim McComb, or about visiting Heaven, or even about my Destiny.

The point of my presentation—in fact, the point of this book—had to be about the Destinies of all of us. I felt compelled to speak about the fact that each of us is born to be the most important person on earth during our lifetime. I can see your eyes rolling as you read this, wondering how each one of the seven billion people on earth could possibly be the *most important person.* Isn't there only *one* "most important person" at any given moment? And even if there *were* more than one, our minds tell us that the important people lead countries, invent new technologies, win Nobel prizes and do other significant things that impact the masses. Most of us *never* expect to be one of *those* important people.

Because we live in a competitive world, we're taught at a very young age that only one person at a time can be the winner, the best, the most important, the one who finishes first. But take time to consider all that you have read in these pages so far and I think you'll agree that each person living today is, in fact, the most important person in the world. If each of us is born with a unique set of skills, talents and abilities, and if each of us is born with an earthbound Personal Destiny that is unique among all Destinies, then we are each here to fulfill a role that no one else can.

If we fail to fulfill that role, then our chair at "the office" is empty and the contribution we were intended to make never materializes because no one else is equipped as precisely as we are to make that contribution. The world winds up missing something that it had to have in order to be complete, something that only you are here to provide. That makes you (and everyone else) the most important person in the world and it makes your Personal Destiny (and everyone else's) the most important responsibility.

So, on the morning of December 6, 2012 I stood at the registration desk for the Business Women Rising Winter Vista Exchange and individually introduced myself to forty different women, just as I will greet you if you ever attend an event at which I am the featured speaker. I grasped each hand, looked deep into each set of eyes and told each of them that they are the most important person in the world, again, just as I will greet you if you ever attend an event at which I am the featured speaker. I do that because the first step in believing that you are the world's most important person is to be told that you are by someone else who believes it. I do.

Transforming the World . . . One Life at a Time

The quote that opened the Preface to this book is attributed to me, and underneath the quote I describe myself as an "ordinary guy." I did that because I wanted every reader to understand that having been to Heaven or having written a book does not make me any more significant a person than you are. Like you, I have a unique combination of divinely-granted assets and like you intend to do, I've identified my earthbound Personal Destiny and am in a focused pursuit to fulfill it.

As I've said over and over, Destiny is about serving others. But in Heaven I discovered that God is truly glorified when you take serving others to an entirely new level by transforming their lives for the better. When that happens, the world becomes a better place than it was yesterday and God smiles.

Often, the transformation of your own life by someone else is the gentle nudge that awakens the power within you to transform others. Most likely, only a handful of people will truly have transformational influence on you in your lifetime. My daughter Laura regenerated my character and altered the course my life, as did Steve Haines (my mentor), Miss Mathews (my junior high English teacher) and my wife Sally. Each of them had evolutionary influence on me; through them, my life transformed over time.

On occasion, someone will shift your thinking in the blink of an eye, inspiring change in your life in a significantly shorter period of time. About ten years ago, I was on the management team of the largest corporate credit union in the United States. Our 80-year-old CEO, Mr. Johnson, was an icon in the credit union industry and had headed our company for a quarter century, following a thirty year career as an officer and decorated war hero in the Marines. He took annual trips to go undersea diving in the most beautiful and challenging places in the world.

I provide this background on Mr. Johnson because it is important for you to know that, even at his advanced age, he was a brilliant, respected and energetic leader. Every one of his three hundred employees respected and revered him; more than a CEO, he was a father figure. The things that he said and did were important to all of us who shared the workday with him.

One day, I was in his office going over a draft of our credit union's strategic plan. As a Marine, Mr. Johnson's career had generally been about tactics—about "taking the hill"—and longer-term strategic planning was sometimes a tough sell for me when I made presentations to him. I wasn't always sure that he thought creating the position of VP of Strategic Planning—the position to which I had been hired—was a good idea. Because he didn't always share everything that he was thinking, I often wondered if he even thought Jim McComb was the right person for the position.

As we sat there on the sofa in his office, he suddenly interrupted me and said, "You make a difference here. I'm glad we hired you." Those two short sentences had more impact on me than any other words spoken to me anywhere, by anyone, during my entire thirty-five year career in business. In one brief moment, a man that I admired, respected and *feared* had confirmed his faith in my ability. He never knew the impact his words had on me, but they inspired me to new heights of productivity and creativity and thought leadership, not only at the credit union, but in virtually everything I have done since that day. Those words have stayed with me, even appearing on my professional resume and on my LinkedIn profile.

Regardless of whether you have evolutionary influence on someone or make a split-second, yet lasting, impact the result is the same. You have the power to make someone else's life better. You've always had that power, and always will have it. The pursuit of your earthbound Personal Destiny gives energy to that power.

I was honored by what Mr. Johnson said to me that day, and felt good about having affected his life in a meaningful way, yet on The Day I Went To Heaven I discovered something of far greater significance: we often never know the extent of the lasting impact we have on those we touch, and it's OK not to know because changing lives, not gathering kudos, is the reason we serve.

During the time I spent in Heaven, the most significant lessons that I witnessed from my past were often events that seemed rather insignificant to me at the time I actually lived them, if I even remembered them at all. Through His eyes, I saw myself walking along a busy downtown street in Portland, Oregon many years ago, where I was approached by a disheveled man looking for money. Normally I ignored such requests, not wanting my hard-earned dollars to feed someone's cigarette habit or contribute to their slide into a wine-induced stupor. Oddly though, on this particular day, I didn't brush the man aside. Instead, I invited him to join me for lunch at a Subway I was heading to at the end of the block.

Although I remembered the incident the moment I saw it re-run before my eyes, I was still just as surprised at the invitation that spilled out of my mouth as I had been when I first issued it that day. I was stunned when the man accepted, but I motioned him alongside me for the short walk to the restaurant. I had expected him to decline, preferring cash to my offer of lunch. Once inside, I ordered a sub, a bag of chips, a cookie and a drink. I told him that I would pay for a similar meal for him, and he ordered.

As we ate, I asked about his life and his situation. His name was Art and he was 36 years old. He had lost his job a few years earlier and descended into depression, costing him his marriage. With that, he took a wad of paper from his pocket and flipped through it, eventually producing dog-eared photos of his wife Sandy and of two young children he said he hadn't seen in years. Art obviously hadn't lived a normal life in a long time, but what really struck me was the look in his eye. I had remembered it all these years, and was seeing it up close once again. It was a wistful look, a melancholy mixture of regret and hopelessness. I saw a man resigned to a fate he didn't choose and paralyzed by the perception that he couldn't do anything about it.

As we sat there preparing to put a wrap on lunch and go our separate ways, I reached into my wallet and pulled out the last bit of cash I had on me that day, about twenty dollars. I slid it across the table toward Art and told him that I wanted to make an investment in his future. He looked surprised and said he didn't have a future. I disagreed and told him that a rewarding future is out there waiting for all of us, and that we just simply have to visualize what we want and go after it. The strategic planner in me was doing the talking because this conversation was years before Undiscovered Horizons was even a twinkle in my eye (or so I thought). I didn't realize at the time how prophetic my response to Art was, not just for him, but for my own life as well.

Parting ways at the restaurant door, we shook hands and I noticed that his countenance had begun to change a bit. As Art disappeared down the block, I also saw that his gait now had a bit of confidence and purpose to it. He looked straight ahead instead of staring at the sidewalk below. He was headed somewhere.

I never saw Art again and didn't know what had happened in his life after that day, until now. Through Christ's eyes, I saw a much-older Art and barely recognized him because the resignation I had seen in his face so long ago was now gone. It was Christmas, and Art was seated in a living room by a beautifully decorated tree with a lady who bore a resemblance to the young woman in the photo he had shown me years earlier. Gathered around the tree, in chairs and on the floor, were his two children, now grown, and their spouses and Art's grandchildren. Smiles had replaced the sadness of the past.

As it turned out, Art had left the Subway that day and walked directly to a rescue mission, where he signed up for counseling and job training. In a few months, he was once again the Art that Sandy had fallen in love with and one day he picked up the telephone. Though I was unaware of it at the time, a lunch and my willingness to invest a few seemingly insignificant dollars in a solitary stranger's future had turned four lives in a different direction.

So, you have the power to transform lives, and you don't have to be famous, or rich, or smart or powerful to do it. That power—or rather, what you do with that power—makes your Personal Destiny unique and shapes the legacy you leave behind when you die. That power is the heart of what makes you The Most Important Person in the World. Believing in your importance unleashes that power.

Perhaps it is our inherent sense of modesty that keeps most of us from believing that we have any measure of importance in the world at all. We get embarrassed when we're complimented by others, we shy away from the spotlight, we would rather follow than lead and we crave a life of obscurity. And if we do ever have the urge to get "out there," we quickly remind ourselves that people who want to be the center of attention have big egos, are conceited, and rarely think of anyone but themselves . . . at least that is what our upbringing has taught most of us.

But do those traits really describe you? Are you really someone who rarely thinks of anyone but yourself? Odds are, you're not. Most parents devote a lifetime to putting the needs of others ahead of their own. Anyone, in any career, who takes their job seriously focuses on someone else's needs the minute a customer calls or walks through the door. If you're a member of a family, or have any friends, or have ever encountered another human being who needs help, I'm guessing that you've put the needs of others ahead of your own on countless occasions over the years.

Obviously, ego-centricity and conceit are traits you never want to see when you look in the mirror, but you must have a confident belief in your abilities and your importance in order to fulfill your God-given purpose. God certainly must believe in the vital nature of your importance or He would not have gifted you with a unique set of skills, abilities and talents that enable you to do something specific that no one else on the earth can do. You trust and glorify and honor God when you believe in yourself and in the importance of what He sent you here to accomplish.

Transforming the World . . . In Your Own Unique Way

Within the context of your newly-discovered Station of Destiny, in what way might *you alone* serve others and change the world? What can *you* do to transform lives and leave the world better off today than it was on the day you were born? Brainstorm a little. Jot down some thoughts, feelings, bullet points, breakthroughs, ideas, reflections, impressions, and any images that come to mind. Write down anything you can think of that might describe the way that you alone will serve people and change the world. Don't allow yourself to weed out the "bad" ideas, because there are none at this point. Don't allow a lack of money, or credentials, or time or any other resource to limit your thinking.

People often ask me for ideas about how to serve people in a manner that will truly make a difference in their lives. While there are literally hundreds of ways to make life better for someone else, a few of the most common ways that come to mind include providing for their basic needs (like food, clothing or shelter), teaching or mentoring them, helping them to achieve a goal or fulfill a purpose, encouraging or inspiring them, being a catalyst for change in their life, promoting or supporting them, running errands for them or providing other kinds of assistance, or simply communicating (listening, sharing, questioning) with them. Some people just want someone to engage them, or include them, or appreciate them, or thank them or love them.

Feel free to take a few days or weeks to think about this, because it is critical. The specific and special ways in which you serve people and change the world are the ingredients in the fulfillment of your purpose. It's *how* you serve others and transform lives, and *how* you leverage your skills, abilities and talents to do it, that makes your earthbound Destiny both unique and Personal to you.

Send your ideas to me at JimMcComb@UndiscoveredHorizons.com. I'd be pleased to see what you've come up with, and to drop you a note back with a few quick ideas of my own.

The Lake of Life

Near the end of my time in Heaven I once again focused, through His eyes, on the river of color that He had called the Fabric of Life. As I studied it, I noticed that the river now flowed into a vast rainbow lake that equaled the river in its stunning brilliance. The lake seemed to have no end and I could not see any of the shoreline as it faded into the distance. Christ cast a large stone into the lake, and as it hit the surface I watched hundreds of ripples emanate from the liquid crater into which the stone had descended from sight.

He said the stone represented my life, the lake was the world and the rainbow "waters" of the surface of the lake—which He called the Lake of Life—represented the lives of all of the people now living in the world. The stone—my life—was gone, symbolizing my departure from the world. Yet the impact of the stone on the surface, representing the impact of my life on the world, continued to generate ripples on the surface long after the stone had disappeared from view. Those ripples symbolized the lasting impact that my life, or the life of anyone who fulfills their earthbound Personal Destiny, will continue to have on humanity after I am gone.

As I watched the ripples continue to travel in vast waves across the surface of the Lake of Life, faces began to materialize in those waves. Jennifer was there, as were Brian, and Katie and Ryan and nearly twenty others. These were the faces of a fourth grade Sunday school class that I had taught in 1982. The faces aged before my eyes, into the forty-year-olds that these kids are today. As I realized that they are parents themselves now, and that perhaps one or more of them might now even be teaching elementary Sunday school, I felt so old!

I also felt an incredible sense of peace and fulfillment. Although most teachers, whether they're in public school, Sunday school or traffic school, rarely ever know if they have any lasting impact on their students, I was about to become one of those rarities.

As the faces and the ripples began to fade, I heard forty-year-old Brian call out in his ten-year-old voice, "Hey Ryan!

Look! Over there! It's Jim! (even as fourth graders, they had called me by my first name) His was the best Sunday school class that we ever had!" Ryan, the class clown, nodded in agreement. After all of these years of not knowing whether I had done anything other than simply keep order amid a roomful of fourth grade chaos, the ripples seemed to confirm it. I had touched tomorrow.

Touching Tomorrow

There is probably no better example of casting ripples in the Lake of Life than those who teach, whether they do it in a public school classroom or in a corporate training room, or sitting on the bed next to their child before lights out. People who teach, even if it's not their formal profession, touch tomorrow. I never realized that until I met a woman named Nora Schliske in the mid 1980's.

I had just been elected to a position on the Salem-Keizer School Board, in Oregon's second largest school district. Nora, a teacher, was the President of the Salem Education Association. She pulled me aside one evening before a board meeting and slipped a lapel pin into the palm of my hand. The pin was a cascading rainbow in vibrant color, much like the river and the lake that I would see many years later in Heaven. On the rainbow were the words *Teachers Touch Tomorrow*.

Nora explained that teachers touch tomorrow because they change the course of history by what they do today. As they ignite a passion for learning and questioning and exploring and experimenting in the minds of their students, teachers set the future in motion for tomorrow's leaders, thinkers, inventors, parents and, yes, for tomorrow's teachers and trainers and home-schooling moms as well. It's true, teachers do touch tomorrow. Nora didn't have to sell me on that notion. She gave me that pin nearly thirty years ago. Not only do I still have it, but it is on my lapel every time I speak to a group—any group—about *Undiscovered Horizons*.

I've seen teachers touch tomorrow in my own life many times. Miss Mathews, the junior high English teacher most responsible for the person I am today, touched tomorrow when she set me on course to fulfill my Destiny way back in the fall of 1966 . . . years before I even knew I had a Destiny. Although she taught me nearly fifty years ago, her work continues to live today through my life even though she has been gone for nearly two decades. Years later in California I dated an elementary school teacher named Lauri who regularly reached into her own purse to finance the purchase of supplies for her classroom and special surprises for her students. She was all about making learning fun and meaningful. Her students were as important to her as her own children, and they knew it. She began teaching many years ago and I have no doubt that her efforts with kids who are now grown are paying dividends to society today.

Teachers and trainers, though, are not the only ones who touch tomorrow. You can too. Connect with people, serve them and transform lives, and you'll become part of a chain of service that extends across generations and touches people you will never know or ever meet. Your footprints will be firmly planted in the future.

Creating Ripples in the Lake of Life

Within the context of your newly-discovered Station of Destiny, in what unique way might *you* create ripples in the Lake of Life? What can *you* do to serve others and to transform lives today that will have a lasting impact for years to come? Again, brainstorm a little. Jot down some thoughts, feelings, bullet points, breakthroughs, ideas, reflections, impressions, and any images that come to mind. Write down anything you can think of that might describe the ripples you will create. Don't allow yourself to weed out the "bad" ideas, because there are none at this point. Don't allow a lack of money, or credentials, or time or any other resource to limit your thinking.

Feel free to take a few days or weeks to think about this, because it is critical. The specific and special ways in which you change the world and create ripples in the Lake of Life are the ingredients in the fulfillment of your purpose. It's *how* you serve others and transform lives, and *how* you leverage your skills, abilities and talents to do it, that makes your earthbound Destiny both unique and Personal to you.

Send your ideas to me at JimMcComb@UndiscoveredHorizons.com. I'd be pleased to see what you've come up with, and to drop you a note back with a few quick ideas of my own.

Finding & Fulfilling Your Destiny: Step Six

In Chapter Ten, you identified, at long last, the Station of Destiny for which God has prepared you, yet it probably didn't seem remotely unique or even very personal. If you believe that many others on the planet share your Station, you would be correct. Millions of people have been prepared to teach, advise, heal or lead others. Simply having a unique set of skills, abilities, talents, chance encounters, coincidental opportunities and persistent notions built around an Intrinsic Gift is not enough to make your Destiny personal *or* unique.

The secret is in how you *apply* that collective group of divinely-granted assets to the way you live your life. In what ways, using those assets, can *you alone* serve others—and change lives—within your Station of Destiny? In what ways, using those assets, can *you alone* create positive change that will continue to impact the lives of others long after you are gone? Answer those questions, and you will know exactly what God intends for you to accomplish during your years on earth.

The **sixth step in finding and fulfilling your own unique Personal Destiny** is identifying and understanding the power that your single, solitary life has in the grand scheme of the world and its future. This understanding is essential to your ability to ultimately fulfill your newfound purpose.

So, God has provided your unique Personal Destiny and the tools to achieve it. You've discovered your Horizon and the Ultimate Destination is now your focus. Life's Most Incredible Odyssey will take you there. The departure date is now up to you.

12

Life's Most Incredible Odyssey

A vision is not just a picture of what could be; it is an appeal to our better selves, a call to be something more.

Rosabeth Moss Kanter (1943-present)
Professor, management consultant, author

When I was in college, I used to make the 1,000 mile journey from Knoxville, Tennessee home to Rockford, Illinois for the holidays each year. Before returning to the classroom grind, thirty or forty of my old friends from various high schools around northern Illinois and southern Wisconsin would come together for an annual reunion on New Year's Eve. We would gather at the home of a widow whose two children were part of our crowd and spend the entire night catching up on what Life had brought each of us during the previous year.

My family moved to Eugene, Oregon in the summer of 1974, so New Year's Eve of 1973 was the last time I attended one of those parties. It was noisy and everyone was partying at full speed. Happiness was everywhere, or so it seemed.

New Year's Eve is a night of hope for some, a time of anticipating hidden future opportunities that will suddenly unveil themselves and beg to be exploited during the year ahead. For others it's a night of despair, spent reflecting on dismal past failures that threaten to cast a shadow over all that lies ahead for months or years to come.

Hope, despair, anticipation and regret. All were present on that night years ago. As I circulated among friends I hadn't seen in several months, three definitive themes began to emerge. For some people, the year ahead was already brimming with goals and projects and promise. They clearly knew where they were going and couldn't wait to get started.

For many more, this New Year's Eve was a night that came too soon because the just-concluded year had offered them too little time to do too many things. Their lives held promise, but were in paralyzed disarray because they just didn't know what to do first. As a result, they often simply did nothing and became demoralized when yet another year passed without any progress.

The others at the party that night had simply sleepwalked through the year without any goals or any regard for what they might have accomplished. Figuratively still asleep, they were destined for yet another lost year. For them, simply getting through each day had been an accomplishment. They wanted no greater challenge for the New Year than that.

In the days that followed, I thought a lot about the people I talked to that night. Some felt a certain sense of fulfillment about the year that had just ended, but seemed to have no idea why. Others felt unfulfilled and clearly knew why. They just couldn't get organized or motivated enough to do anything of real value with their lives, at least not yet.

Perhaps the greatest number of people I talked to that night were in the most unenviable position of all. They also felt unfulfilled, but were clueless as to why they felt that way. The New Year held no promise for them; Life had no meaning for them. They were adrift, with no sense of purpose or direction. Even the Christians in that group—those most likely to feel fulfilled and have a sense of purpose because of their relationship with Christ—seemed to have a sense of uncertainty about where the future was taking them.

As the hour approached midnight, it would soon be another year. For most at the party, it would be just that . . . another year. But the few who knew the secret to success were destined for a special year . . . *their* year.

Christ directed my attention to a road that had its beginning beyond the Horizon, beyond the point at which those who have searched for it will ultimately discover their earthbound Personal Destiny. Through His eyes, I saw that the road was actually a rainbow nestled in a cloud and it reminded me of the Fabric of Life that I had seen earlier, carrying new souls to earth and to the beginning of their own lives. The road mimicked the Fabric of Life in that it was made from colors so vivid, so intense, and so vibrant that they clearly seemed to be alive. As I had previously observed, many of the rainbow's colors were hues I had never seen at any time during my life on earth. But one of the most prominent elements in the rainbow was a color (though not really a color) with which I was very familiar, although I had never before seen it in a rainbow. One of the strands, woven among the glowing threads of color, was pure white.

Vast numbers of people were walking this "rainbow road"—women and children and men of all ages, races and stations in Life—each headed toward their own Ultimate Destination, toward the fulfillment of something they had each been fortunate to have already discovered . . . their unique earthbound Personal Destiny. Among the enormous throng, I spotted a few of the friends, neighbors, co-workers and family members who have been a part of my nearly sixty years of life. All of those I recognized are still alive on the earth today, fully engaged in what God calls Life's Most Incredible Odyssey, the quest for fulfillment that logically follows arrival at the Horizon. Some of you who are now reading these words were among those I saw setting out on this Odyssey, walking the "rainbow road."

Christ now explained to me that the road I was seeing through His eyes was simply an extension of the same Fabric of Life I had seen earlier, carrying new souls to life on earth. The white strand in the rainbow was Righteousness . . . the influence of God on the direction of those who are walking that radiant road. It became clear to me as I watched the throng that even though the journey is choreographed by God, the travelers were each calculating their own deliberate steps, like dancers interpreting, in their own way, the vision of their Heavenly choreographer.

Each of us who discovers his or her Personal Destiny walks this important pathway, undertaking Life's Most Incredible Odyssey, at some point during our lifetime, although we never see it. You might be traveling that road at this very moment and every step you take will be calculated and deliberate, just as those of the travelers I saw through His eyes. But taking those steps requires careful planning because, although it is true that God has an ultimate plan for you, that "free will" thing is always on the prowl waiting to divert you away from your destination. Since you'll find the same exits on your Odyssey that were on the road to your Undiscovered Horizon, you'll need a Destiny Plan to keep yourself focused on arriving at your Ultimate Destination at the right time and in the right place. A Destiny Plan is like a personal strategic plan, but unlike other plans you'll make during the course of your lifetime.

Most of us make plans to achieve grand goals in our lives by making resolutions on New Year's Eve or by blowing out the candles in celebration of yet another birthday. Most often though, we simply plant an informal plan in our mind that ultimately gets lost amid the millions of thoughts that occupy the obscure recesses of our brain.

Ultimately, the most important plan you will ever make is the one that comes in the wake of discovering your unique mission on earth . . . the one that determines how you will navigate the rainbow while on your Odyssey, and when you will arrive at your Ultimate Destination . . . the fulfillment of your earthbound

Personal Destiny. That plan must be written down. It must be woven into your life every day and it must be more important than anything else in your life, except your faith and your family.

The *Undiscovered Horizons Personal Destiny Plan* workbook is an excellent resource to help you organize that plan and bring it into focus. Whether you use the workbook or not, the time to begin thinking about your plan is right now. Fulfilling your Destiny involves divine guidance from God and a bit of strategic thinking by you. Your Destiny Plan is a mixture of the two and has been coming together the entire time you've been reading this book.

Strategic thinking is thinking that relates what you do today to who you (and God) want you to become tomorrow, and helps you make vital choices about how to allocate your time, money and energy. Your Destiny Plan answers two fundamental questions, "What can, or should, I do today to ensure that I will fulfill my Destiny and glorify God, honoring the earthbound purpose He chose for me?" *and* "If a particular event occurs in my life today, how will that impact my ability to fulfill my Personal Destiny?"

As you contemplate your Destiny Plan, refer to the things you've thought about and the notes you've made about your own life as you've read this book and shared the journey I took to find and fulfill my own Destiny. As you develop your Destiny Plan, write it down. Use the *Undiscovered Horizons Personal Destiny Plan* workbook, a piece of notebook paper or the back of a used junk mail envelope. Use anything. Just use *something,* because a written plan is more powerful than one you try to commit to memory. When your plan is in front of you, things happen because it's in your face every day. It challenges you to move the needle, to achieve, and to ultimately fulfill the Destiny that the rest of us are waiting for you to fulfill. A copy in the hands of a spouse, a partner or a friend can be a powerful tool of accountability.

Determine to succeed. Take one small step every day. A fifteen minute daily commitment makes a significant difference and fulfills Destiny. Revise your plan as the rainbow takes you in new directions. Surround yourself with supportive people, with people who themselves believe in Personal Destiny, with people who will be resources along your Odyssey. Stay at it, every day. Make progress, every day. Celebrate your progress every day. Oliver Wendell Holmes once said that most of us go to our graves with our music still inside us. Resolve not to be one of those people.

Navigating the Rainbow . . . Life's Most Incredible Odyssey

When you think of a Destiny Plan, visualize a road map or the GPS screen in your car. A map shows you where to go, what you'll encounter along the way, and allows you to calculate about how long it will take to get there. A Destiny Plan fulfills a similar role. The Plan's components work in a logical sequence to take you along the rainbow, step by step, to the Ultimate Destination, to be "something better."

As you prepare to write your Personal Destiny Plan, think first about those people in your life who will be impacted by the fulfillment of your Destiny. They might include your spouse or partner, your children, your parents, brothers and sisters, in-laws, grandparents, aunts and uncles, the clergy at your house of worship, your mentor, your employer, personal advisors (such as your attorney, your doctor or your financial advisor), co-workers, friends, neighbors and, if you have them, your customers or clients. In what specific way will each of these people be impacted by your pursuit of your Personal Destiny? In what ways can they help you? In what ways might they hinder you? What role does each ultimately play in the fulfillment of your Destiny? Which of them should be involved with you in the development of your plan? Which of them might have responsibilities to meet in order for you to fulfill your Destiny?

In the six Appendices to this book you'll find important background on each of the six components of your Destiny Plan. The *Undiscovered Horizons Personal Destiny Plan* workbook is a place to find the templates and forms for the structure of your plan so that you don't have to invent the wheel yourself.

I've included the bulk of the information on the structure of a plan in the Appendices of this book. This material used to be a part of this chapter, but my wife told me after reading it that, while it is important and needed information that includes more of my experiences in Heaven, it made the chapter too long and "interrupted the flow of the book." I re-read it and agreed, so it became an easy call to move that part of the chapter to the Appendices. Please be aware, though, that fulfilling your Personal Destiny without reading that information will be difficult because it's the map that helps you navigate the rainbow and successfully complete your Odyssey.

Below are the brief basics of each of the six Destiny Plan components. An appendix is devoted to each one and provides additional depth that you'll need, more about my experiences in Heaven and a few more stories.

Life Mission (Station of Destiny): Your Station of Destiny is your Life Mission—the basic, fundamental purpose of your life—what you do, for whom you do it, and the value or benefit that others derive from what you do. It's the role that you were born to play . . . your reason for being. Some mission statements articulate core values, beliefs, philosophies, core competencies and capabilities. None of these areas, however, are appropriate for a Life Mission. It simply defines your purpose. Nothing more. Nothing less.

Vision (Ultimate Destination): Your Vision is your imagined view of how the world actually looks on a specific date in the future once you have fulfilled your Life Mission. Typically written in present tense as a one-paragraph narrative story, your Vision succinctly and specifically describes what your Life Mission looks like in its fulfilled state. Vision is the lynchpin of your Plan, and of your life, because it is your *Ultimate Destination*. For you, it defines ultimate success.

Success Measures (Goals): Success measures are calculable outcome measures of the progress you're making (goals you're achieving) toward the fulfillment of your earthbound Personal Destiny. These measures should be ones for which you can physically see progress. You should know objectively whether or not they have been achieved. Measures are important because without them it is impossible to quantify the difference you're making in the world, and quantifying that difference is important because measurable progress keeps you motivated and focused. When others see visible progress, they're more likely to support your journey and to walk along with you.

Strategies (Life's Most Incredible Odyssey): Strategies are paths of action that collectively contribute to the realization of your Vision. They are based on your Success Measures and are generally expressed as proactive statements describing the approach to achieving the various outcomes that are inherent in your Vision. The strategies you ultimately choose are important because they become the key priorities around which you allocate your time, money, energy, ideas and other assets.

Tactics (Action Steps): Tactics are the action steps that you take along your Odyssey that lead to fulfillment of your Vision and your earthbound Personal Destiny. Completed Tactics mean a fulfilled Destiny. Each of your Strategies will have at least one action step, and usually more than one. Completing some action steps actually prompts the addition of new tactics to your to-do list, while others are added simply because you didn't think of them when you initially developed your Destiny Plan.

Tactics include a clear statement of the <u>exact action to be taken</u>, a specific <u>timeframe</u> within which the action will be taken or a <u>deadline</u> by which it will be completed (put all beginning and ending dates on your personal calendar so that your Tactics will become a part of your day-to-day to-do list), the name of the person (usually your name, but occasionally a family member or personal advisor) who has ultimate <u>accountability</u> for completing the action step, and any hard cost (<u>cash outlay or tangible resource</u>) or soft cost (<u>time or intangible resource</u>) necessary to complete it.

Evaluating Progress (Destiny Evolution): The evaluation step is essentially a progress check that you make on a regular basis to determine whether or not you're on track to fulfill your Destiny within the parameters you've set for yourself. If you're not on track, this is the point at which you determine why you're not and what you plan to do about it. Most months, though, you'll find yourself generally where you're supposed to be and no corrective action will be needed.

I've become an expert in each of these six areas during a lifetime of passions and pastimes, chance encounters, coincidental opportunities, persistent notions and professional experience. Counseling and advising others is my Intrinsic Gift and is at the heart of what God has asked me to share with you. Many of you have been planning for the fulfillment of your Personal Destiny for most of your life, even if you didn't realize it until you first opened *Undiscovered Horizons.*

Finding & Fulfilling Your Destiny: Step Seven

When I was a child, our family took to the road every summer for a vacation. Yellowstone, New England, Hollywood, Canada and Washington DC were just a few of the destinations we journeyed to from our home in Rockford, Illinois. Inevitably we would find ourselves on the road looking for a motel because my dad hadn't made a reservation. We would pass numerous "No Vacancy" signs and my dad would try to placate us with assurances that "there will be a vacancy in the next town." We always did find a place, but usually it was too late to enjoy a swim in the motel pool or a leisurely dinner. We would arrive just in time for fast food from the last open place in town, followed by lights out.

My dad was generally a planner throughout his life, except when it came to the family vacations we took when I was a kid. Consequently, late afternoons and evenings on the road usually turned into disappointing, stressful and angry times during what were otherwise great vacations. Planning was the weak link, just as it is for most of us. We look back at our careers, our education, our finances, our health, our marriages and our lives in general, and often wish we had planned things a bit better.

When it comes to your Destiny, planning is critical. **The seventh step in finding and fulfilling your own unique Personal Destiny** is carefully planning the goals and the steps that lead you to the Ultimate Destination . . . fulfillment of your Destiny.

While it is true that things happen in your life for a reason and that significant people and opportunities are purposefully injected into your life by God, He won't do all of the work. As long as we have free will, fulfilling our Destiny is a matter of the choices we decide to make in life. A carefully thought-out plan ensures that we will make the choices that lead to the right place, at the right time.

And so the time has finally come. You've discovered the Horizon. You know why you're here, and you know what to do. All that remains is to do it.

Remember that the key to success is to trust God. He'll give us speed bumps throughout our Odyssey, but we must be thankful for every opportunity and every challenge. God puts them in our path to help us succeed, and to ensure that you and I never feel *entitled* to achieve a strategy or to fulfill our earthbound Personal Destiny. God will grant that to each of us in His time.

13

The Ultimate Destination

You can never cross the ocean unless you have the courage to lose sight of the shore.

Christopher Columbus (1451-1506)
Maritime explorer, navigator, colonizer

You are the most important person in the *entire* world! You are the most important person because the world desperately needs what you have. The day you were born, you came out of the womb already prepared to fulfill a very specific purpose . . . a purpose that is unique to *you* . . . a purpose that *only* you can accomplish . . . a purpose that must be realized in *your* lifetime in order for the world to work properly. Because of this, *you* are the most important person on the planet today.

It has been said that the two most significant days in your life are the day you were born, and the day you find out why. *Today* is that second day in your life, because *today* you chose to read this book. You joined me on that extraordinary journey that I took in the summer of 2011, and as you traveled with me you came to realize that this book is really about your own extraordinary journey. You came to realize why you are so important to the rest of us who inhabit the world right now, and to those who will come in the future.

Today is a transformational day for you. Today is your opportunity to begin *living* like the most important person in the world. By reading this book, you've begun *The Incredible Odyssey* (the journey to fulfill your Personal Destiny) because you've discovered your *Horizon* (the reason you're here). Now it's time to move beyond that Horizon, to shift your *Odyssey* into high gear by following your Destiny Plan and to make progress toward the *Ultimate Destination*—the fulfillment of your Personal Destiny. Except for salvation, there is no greater prize in a human lifetime than the unbridled exhilaration that comes from fulfilling your God-given purpose on this earth.

A Farewell to Heaven (for now)

Although today is a transformational day for you, I sense that you're now feeling a bit overwhelmed by what you've read and by the tremendous responsibility you've discovered that you have. If you're overwhelmed, I certainly understand. Although it all seemed so logical and easy to comprehend while I was learning through Christ's eyes, so much was coming at me that I became concerned about remembering it all and about correctly communicating all that I had been shown.

Concern and worry are alien concepts in Heaven, so Christ responded quickly at the first sign that anxiety was beginning to overtake me. Through His eyes, I returned to the fourth floor of the office building in Pasadena where I had begun working ten years ago. On the job scarcely more than three weeks, I observed myself still at work even though the hour was approaching midnight and everyone else had gone home. In a few short hours, the company's draft strategic plan was due to senior management and I was miles behind because very little of the work on the plan had been completed prior to my first day at the company.

I had seven different printers on three different floors cranking out pages of the massive plan while I ran up and down multiple flights of stairs filling paper trays and sending new print jobs to the various printers. Several thousand pages—some of it in color—needed to be printed, collated and bound before I could make the twenty five mile trip home. I was exhausted and overwhelmed, but I kept scurrying from floor to floor and machine to machine because I knew I would never finish in time unless I focused more on taking action and less on thinking about how difficult the task was.

But it seemed that no matter how quickly I worked, my progress was still slow. There were just too many places to be at the same time. There were paper jams in some of the printers, and my computer crashed twice. Just as my frustration began to mount, a woman appeared out of the shadows and asked if I needed help. She said her name was Anna and that she had stopped at the office to pick up something on her way home from somewhere. She plunged in to help without saying another word and we finished that gargantuan task in just over an hour.

Without her help, I would have been there until the wee hours of the morning. That night, since I had never seen her before, I was convinced that she was an angel because she had literally appeared from nowhere without a sound. But now, as I watched my exhausted self finish the last of the project, He revealed that she was simply a co-worker whose path had been directed my way that night.

The point is that when we're overwhelmed and we ask God for help (as I did that night), He provides it. His attention to your needs is particularly acute when you're fulfilling the specific purpose for which He created you. While your Destiny might look too difficult or too challenging, God is ready and waiting to help you. All you have to do is take the first step. Make the effort. Accept the challenge. Do the work. He'll be there to support you, and to reward you.

I'm not sure how long I was in Heaven. It seemed like hours, yet I was gone from this earth for only a few minutes. Time seems to move in weird patterns in the Lord's House, slowing to a crawl at times, and then moving swiftly as if God "winks" us into the future. But no matter how fast or slow time appeared to move, there always seemed to be an urgency to God's tone as He spoke to me. I sensed that obedience was an imperative the entire time I was there. For me, Destiny wasn't an option. It was vital that I clearly understood what I was to do, and that I share what I had learned with others as quickly as possible.

Just as I fully understood the urgency and importance of my mission, the hour of my appointed departure came and I abruptly slipped from within the body of Christ. Once again, I found myself gazing into His stunning, mesmeric eyes. He smiled reassuringly and reached out with His right hand to touch my forehead. In contrast to the softness I had discovered when I first touched His cheek, I now experienced the firm presence of His hand on my forehead. It was a touch of guidance like that of a father to a child . . . a reassuring touch that sent me on my way confident of the direction I had been given, free from fear and uncertainty, with a reassurance that I would return again someday.

I was at peace and as a feeling of deep, abiding love washed over me I was suddenly aware that I was lying on some type of bed in a hallway. Then I felt movement as the bed began to roll. I drifted in and out of consciousness as the bed glided along and I remember talking to someone, although I can't recall who it was or what was said. My consciousness fully returned when I arrived in my room. My wife was there, as were my memories of arriving at the hospital and of the reason I was there. I was back.

The memories of The Day I Went To Heaven were with me as well, vivid replays in stunning detail that are still with me nearly two years later. Unsure that anyone would take me seriously, I kept these memories to myself for more than nine months, preferring to wait until I was sure that I was actually capable of doing what I had been asked to do.

To Believe You Can Is Everything

Months later, long after I had left the hospital, I remained in a state of paralyzed awe whenever I contemplated what had happened to me. Even though I left Heaven with a clear understanding of the responsibility I carried back to my life here, I often had thoughts of inadequacy. Why had I been chosen for this particular experience? There were certainly smarter people—and definitely more righteous people—to whom God could have entrusted this assignment. What if the steps I took to fulfill my Personal Destiny (such as writing this book) failed to inspire or motivate others? I just didn't have faith in my own abilities to pull off what I had been asked to do.

Just as I have questioned my own capability to fulfill my purpose, you probably have some doubt now that you have discovered your own tremendous responsibility. Your first thought is most likely to dismiss your purpose as too time consuming and difficult. You don't have the time, or the energy, or perhaps even the intellectual capacity to do it. If your earthbound Personal Destiny seems overwhelming, too difficult or too unrealistic, just remember that God gave you that Destiny and the tools to fulfill it. He believes in you and obviously thinks you *can* do it, but *you* have to believe you can do it too. When you believe in God, you must therefore believe in yourself. And when you believe in yourself, miracles occur. Consider this story:

You're a major league baseball pitcher with a 1-6 won-loss record and an earned run average way over 5.00. Neither statistic is a sure ticket to the Hall of Fame. It's August 30, your team is in last place and the World Series is barely more than a month away. Your teammates have largely written off the season, but you believe that your team can not only escape last place, but win your division and the National League pennant, and get to the World Series. The phrase "Ya Gotta Believe" pops into your head and you repeat it over and over and over in the dugout, in the clubhouse, on the field and in media interviews. Your team's record is 62-71. "Ya Gotta Believe" that you'll get to the World Series because that's the only way you'll get there.

The next day, on August 31, you win just your second game of the entire season by beating the St. Louis Cardinals in extra innings because you believe. The win moves your team out of last place. Suddenly you're not the only one on the team who believes in a World Series appearance. Others start to listen to you and begin to believe. Three weeks after languishing in last place, your team moves into first place. A few days later, on the final day of the season, you and your teammates win the National League East championship. During that last month of the season, your team went 20-8, you won three more games without a loss and had an earned run average of less than 1.00. Because you believed, others believed, and because they believed, twenty five guys achieved what seemed virtually impossible only a few weeks earlier.

To get to the World Series your team first had to defeat the feared National League West champion Cincinnati Reds, winners of the National League pennant two of the previous three years. Your team played them twelve times during the regular season and only won four of those games. Their overall season record was seventeen games better than your team's record. Yet again, you told your teammates that "Ya Gotta Believe." They did, and you won.

In the World Series that year, your team faced the defending World Series champion Oakland Athletics. Their overall season record was twelve games better than your team's. Once again, you roamed the clubhouse chanting "Ya Gotta Believe." The team believed, and won three of the first five Series games. You (relief pitcher Tug McGraw) were the winning pitcher in Game Two. Although the Athletics ultimately won the Series four games to three, your last-place team (the 1973 New York Mets) made it to the World Series and took one of the best teams of the entire decade to the full seven games before bowing out.

It would have been easy for the Mets to have folded their tent on August 30 because the obstacles to success were too great. It would be easy, too, for you to close this book and never look back, because fulfilling Destiny takes time and passion and commitment. The Mets chose to play. Will you?

The Smallest Thing is the Key

Near the end of my lengthy struggle to write this book, my wife Sally and I took a trip back to Rockford, Illinois to attend my 40th high school reunion. We spent an enjoyable couple of days in Rockford attending the reunion activities and reconnecting with friends I had not seen in four decades. We spent a day in and around Janesville, Wisconsin, another boyhood home of mine, and during our final day in Illinois we drove south to Dixon to tour a home Ronald Reagan had lived in as a boy.

After the tour ended I walked around the home to shoot some pictures while Sally sat in the yard on a bench. Before long a woman came by and the two of them began to make small talk. During the course of the conversation, the woman mentioned that she and a friend planned to have lunch at a restaurant in nearby White Pines State Park. Sally shared that we planned to have Chicago-style pizza in a restaurant in downtown Dixon. They chatted until I came along, and then we went our separate ways.

Later that day, around noon, we were hungry and went in search of the pizza restaurant, only to find it locked. As it turned out, we were in Dixon on the one day of the week, Wednesday, when they were closed. Sally remembered the restaurant in the park, and we soon found ourselves traveling down a country road past miles of farm fields in search of the park. My family had spent many Sunday afternoons at White Pines while I was growing up and it had been nearly fifty years since I had been there. I was curious, because I couldn't remember a restaurant.

We found the park, and the restaurant, and my memories came back to me. The restaurant was in a log lodge that was surrounded by small cabins for rent. After lunch, we went for a walk in the park and eventually sat down in two Adirondack chairs near one of the cabins. As we sat there listening to the peaceful rustling of the trees, I speculated that such a setting—a quiet cabin the woods—would be the perfect place to finish my book. Sally agreed and nothing more was said.

A month later, out of the blue, Sally told me that she had made arrangements to use some of her savings to rent a cabin for me in the California mountains so I could be alone with my computer to finish this book. That is exactly what happened, all because we had a conversation outside a cabin that wasn't ours, after eating lunch in a place we had never intended to go, after talking to a woman we never knew we would meet.

A chance encounter? A coincidence? Call it what you will, but this book was finished when it was largely because my wife happened to be sitting on a bench 2,000 miles from our home at precisely the same instant that a woman she didn't know stopped for a moment to chat. I can't thank the woman for the restaurant suggestion because we don't know her name or where she lives. She was just an anonymous face in the crowd of Life who had an impact on the writing of this book and, therefore, on the fulfillment of my Destiny.

What small thing is waiting to occur in your life? What will be the catalyst for the fulfillment of *your* Destiny?

The Ultimate Destination

Fulfilling Destiny is a scary proposition for most people because there is a certain accountability to it. Once you begin the journey there is an inherent obligation to finish it, but the road is often difficult and it becomes easy to question whether or not you have the talent, the passion or the stamina to finish the race.

Martha Graham, a dancer and choreographer who is considered one of the pioneers of modern dance, once had a close friend confess that she was "bewildered and worried that my entire scale of values was untrustworthy." While she had an intense desire to be an excellent dancer, she in fact had no faith in her ability to deliver. Martha calmed her fears by putting them into the context of Destiny with these words:

> *There is a vitality, a life force, a quickening, that is translated through you into action, and because there is*

only one of you in all of time, this expression is unique. And if you block it, it will never exist through any other medium and it will be lost. The world will not have it.

In just a few sentences, Graham describes Personal Destiny perfectly, reinforces the uniqueness of each person's Destiny, provides us with reason enough to care whether or not we have a Destiny, and tells us what will happen if we fail to seek and fulfill it. In my view, these are some of the most powerful words ever written about Destiny and each one of us should take them as a call to action.

Although many people see fulfillment as doing what they love, or doing what they're passionate about, or doing what makes them the most money with the least effort, real fulfillment far exceeds any of those. It's the payoff, the finish line, the *Ultimate Destination*. It glorifies God because His purpose for your life is achieved, and it delivers a reward to you that is more meaningful than any amount of money, fame or power could ever provide.

As you pursue the fulfillment of your Destiny, you'll develop a stronger faith and a closer bond with God, and you'll trust in Him more completely. Your life will become more focused and disciplined; you'll be at peace more often and will enjoy a heightened level of self-esteem. Relationships will be more meaningful for you, and opportunities and resources will come to you more easily. You'll be filled with vision, energy and contagious optimism. You will find yourself in the right place, at the right time, doing the right thing, with the right people. God will be enthusiastically in your corner.

Real fulfillment is a lifestyle, and for you it will be a full-blown life transformation. You will feel genuinely different because you're doing what you were created to do, and you'll fall asleep every night knowing that you were the person you needed to be, every minute of that day. This is probably why God considers your journey to the *Ultimate Destination* to be *Life's Most Incredible Odyssey.*

You Never Know

When I was a teenager, I lived life with a certain sense of invincibility. I knew that everyone died eventually, and even experienced that first-hand when my maternal grandfather died when I was just fourteen, although I couldn't quite see that day ever coming for me. Planning for retirement, or anything else long-term, was difficult to do because my focus was short-term. In my mind, I had forever to make my mark on the world . . . to make a difference. I wasn't sure what that difference would be, but it didn't matter because I had all the time in the world. I had *forever*.

Right up until The Day I Went To Heaven, I continued to live with that same sense of immortality and invincibility. But it's amazing how a sudden confrontation with your own transience can tend to drive an abrupt search for your purpose, and an immediate concern for the legacy you'll leave behind someday. As I now approach sixty, I realize something that I never quite "got" when I was younger . . . that the most precious commodity that exists in Life is not money. It is time.

We spend a lifetime exchanging money for goods and services that break, go out of style, or are eventually fully consumed, but we don't mind because, for most of us, as long as we have our health and some measure of ingenuity there will always be opportunities to make more money. Time, on the other hand, is more valuable. It buys memories that last forever in our minds and in the minds of those whose lives we touch and improve in some way. But unlike money, there is no opportunity to increase our personal inventory of time.

What you do every day from this point forward has to matter, because you're trading in twenty-four hours of the rest of your life in order to do it. The challenge is that you never know how much you have left of that precious inventory.

Three dozen of those who graduated from high school with me in 1972 are now gone, including two of our class presidents. My childhood best friend died suddenly a few weeks ago at the age of fifty-eight. The first girl I ever dated was killed in an automobile crash while on vacation with her family twenty years ago. She was in her thirties at the time. One of my sister's neighborhood playmates died of leukemia when she was only five. My mother's older brother was only three days old when he died. Time offers us no guarantees, only encouragement to take action now.

Since The Day I Went To Heaven, I've made a commitment to live life more meaningfully and more purposefully. I recommitted my life to Christ, am spending more quality time with friends and family, and have finished this book so that I can begin to fulfill my own Destiny (and ultimately help you to fulfill yours). I've dumped a laundry list of bad habits, time-wasters and miscellaneous distractions from my life in order to re-focus on what is really important while I still have the time.

After all, You Never Know . . .

Your Time is Now

My mom and dad were both wonderful people who did many remarkable things during their lifetimes. Yet, in spite of their accomplishments, neither of them did all they wanted to, or needed to. They were on this earth for a combined 146 years, yet—like the vast majority of those who lived before them—neither ever knew why they were born or what their real purpose in Life was. As a result, neither of them ever completed their purpose. Tragically, history loses something significant every time someone misses the opportunity to discover and fulfill their Personal Destiny.

My parents, and perhaps yours as well, are gone now. Their moments have passed, but yours has not. For you, that moment is right here. Right now. Today, you're the most important person in the *entire* world. God gave you have a unique Personal Destiny that no one else can fulfill and the future of world, literally, depends on you. What you have to share will make a genuine difference in the lives of others, and God is counting on you to deliver.

So are people you don't even know. They're counting on you to take action *today* to fulfill your own Destiny. Someone in a homeless shelter in Chicago is counting on you, as are a wealthy business owner in Belgium, a student at a college in Portland, a farmer in rural China, a struggling family in Knoxville, a newborn baby in Peru, and a young entrepreneur in Denver. I'm counting on you. So are my wife and my daughter and step-daughter. We're just a few of the millions of people around the world who are counting on you. You don't know us, and we don't know you, but our future depends on what you decide to do *today*.

We're waiting for what *you* have to share.

Appendix A

Life Mission

Life Mission (Station of Destiny)

Your Station of Destiny is your Life Mission—the basic, fundamental purpose of your life—what you do, for whom you do it, and the value or benefit that others derive from what you do. It's the role that you were born to play . . . your reason for being. Some mission statements articulate core values, beliefs, philosophies, core competencies and capabilities. None of these areas, however, are appropriate for a Life Mission. It simply defines your purpose. Nothing more. Nothing less.

Your Life Mission is defined by the common thread that is woven throughout your core values, passions and pastimes, chance encounters, coincidental opportunities, persistent notions, and core and secondary intrinsic gifts. Following that thread throughout Chapter Ten led you to discover your Station of Destiny and to translate it into a personalized Life Mission unique to you in Chapter Eleven.

Your Destiny Plan begins with that mission, which is essentially a clear, concise, one-sentence description of your earthbound Personal Destiny. That single sentence is an important one. In just a handful of words, it answers a collective set of questions that define why you're here.

Who are you? Why do you exist? Whom do you serve? What do you do for those you serve? How do you make their lives better? What do you offer? Help? Hope? Knowledge? A listening ear or a comforting shoulder? Guidance? Inspiration? Accountability? A fresh start? Appreciation? Engagement and passion? Support? Inclusion? The list of possible contributions you could make to someone else's life is endless. But no matter how long that list might get, one thing will always be certain. Every item on it is a way to make life better for someone else.

Sit quietly now and ponder these questions as they apply to your life and to your own earthbound Personal Destiny. Take all the time you need because your thoughts over the next few minutes will eventually come together in the creation of one of the most important sentences you have ever written. One solitary sentence—Your Life Mission—is the very foundation upon which the fulfillment of your Destiny is built. Nothing can stand without a proper foundation. Not your home. Not your marriage. Not the fulfillment of your Personal Destiny.

Begin to brainstorm answers to the questions and jot them down on paper as soon as they come to you. Look for common themes and put those themes in a mini-outline so that your thoughts will be easier to organize into a single sentence. Reflect on the Personal Destiny you discovered and defined in Chapters Ten and Eleven.

If you'd like an example to follow, please allow me to share my Life Mission with you. As you may remember, my earthbound Personal Destiny is to help others (you, and the other readers of this book) discover and fulfill their own Destinies. Reflecting on that, I defined my Life Mission this way:

Appendix A

I exist to inspire and prepare ordinary people in all walks of Life to accomplish extraordinary things through discovering, and fulfilling, their own unique Personal Destinies.

After you've written your Life Mission, re-read it several times to ensure that it truly defines your mission on this earth. Does that one sentence clearly and concisely identify the reason you exist? Does it identify those whose lives you are working to make better? Does it identify specifically what you do, and the outcome you seek to produce?

Your Life Mission should also meet each of the seven "Rules of the Road" that were introduced in Chapter Three in order to confirm that is has grown out of a Destiny that is truly genuine. First, it should be a mission that you believe in your heart is divinely inspired and supported. It also must fundamentally focus on service to others, and apply your skills, abilities and talents to achieve an end that is unique to you. Your mission should be a test of faith that requires focus and a full investment of both your life and talent, trumping everything except your faith and your family. It should encompass all aspects of your life and not be limited just to your career or profession and finally—and most importantly—it must offer you ultimate fulfillment.

If your Life Mission statement effectively addresses each of the questions and criteria above, it is ready to be the foundation for the fulfillment of your Personal Destiny. Please share it with me at JimMcComb@UndiscoveredHorizons.com. I would be honored to be one of the first to know your Life Mission.

Appendix B

Vision

Vision (Ultimate Destination)

Your Vision is your imagined view of how the world actually looks on a specific date in the future once you have fulfilled your Life Mission. Typically written in present tense as a one-paragraph narrative story, your Vision succinctly and specifically describes what your Life Mission looks like in its fulfilled state. Vision is the lynchpin of your Plan, and of your life, because it is your *Ultimate Destination*. For you, it defines ultimate success.

Stations of Destiny are general and generic, and many others no doubt share your Station. What makes your Personal Destiny unique is that it is your inimitable way of living your Station in the service of others, combined with your distinctive way of using the one-of-a-kind combination of intrinsic gifts you were given to create ripples in the Lake of Life and change the world.

<u>Vision comes from the heart</u>, that place where passion dwells. Although we always think of romantic passion in connection with the heart, the passion that actually lives there is an unfettered

yearning that drives us to do those vitally important things in life (like fulfilling our Personal Destiny) that we often don't want to do because we're convinced they're too difficult and time-consuming to achieve. No matter how insurmountable the odds are or how little time you have, the things you're passionate about manage to get done. And they're done well, with your full devotion and attention, because you care deeply about them and are committed to them.

I once worked with an accounting clerk named Katherine who had two young children and a failing marriage. She knew that her life was about to change in ways that wouldn't lead to the future she had always envisioned for her children. Realizing that education was the key to that future, she went back to school in pursuit of a bachelor's degree. It wasn't easy. Life became an endless stream of grueling days filled with work and classes and studying, punctuated by the responsibilities of being a single parent. The joys of everyday life that we all take for granted were suddenly gone.

Although her mind was the critical element in making each day a success at work, at school and at home, it was the vision embedded in her heart that made that success possible. Her love for her children, her passionate desire to be something more than an accounting clerk and her commitment to the future of her dreams were the drivers of her ultimate success. Without the necessary link between passion and vision, she would have collapsed in an exhausted heap long before completing her degree program (which, by the way, she did complete) or realizing her vision (today she enjoys a new job, a new level of self-respect, and the prospect of the future she wanted for her family).

<u>Vision also comes from the farthest edges of your imagination</u>, as it must, because it is imagination that has brought us all of history's greatest innovations and inventions and ideas. Imagination is God teasing and challenging your mind to find a better way, to go farther, to think differently and to do things never tried or accomplished before. Without imagination, you put limits on God and on the miracles He is waiting to accomplish through you.

Without imagination, you're likely to say, "That's good enough," instead of "That's not enough."

How fortunate we are that history has brought us a steady parade of people who used their imaginations to move beyond "good enough." Thanks to those imaginations, we're beneficiaries of the wheel, television, the Internet, light bulbs, the personal computer, air travel, the telephone, paper, the camera, disease cures, the printing press, democracy, the internal combustion engine and social networks. Decades from now, our grandchildren will use imagination to create wonders that today are beyond our wildest dreams. Imagination will always be a primary source of Vision.

Obviously, because your Vision is the fulfillment of your Personal Destiny, it is necessarily <u>unique to you</u> and your life, is <u>focused on service to others</u>, and is <u>consistent with your newfound definition of success</u>. But if your Vision is truly authentic, and if it is a legitimate representation of your Personal Destiny, then you must be able to recognize other qualities in it as well. Genuine Vision is bold, compelling, inspiring, radical, embarrassing and measurable.

<u>Vision is bold</u> because it has to be. Boldness is a departure from life's norm. People who are bold do things differently from the way others do them; they imagine the impossible and then they muster the courage to accomplish it. Regardless of whether the impossible is ever achieved, the incidental discoveries they make along the way still make positive contributions to changing the course of human existence.

The explorers who left Europe and Asia to blaze new trails in Africa and in North and South America envisioned worlds none of their contemporaries had ever seen. They risked disease, fear, unforgiving seas, food shortages, weather and a host of other challenges, all in bold pursuit of streets of gold, fountains of youth, new trade routes and untouched worlds of beauty and splendor . . . Visions that few of those they left behind believed were real. The explorers, inventors, architects, innovators and builders of the present day take risks too, with money, with time and ideas, and even with relationships. All of the great advances of our time in medicine, energy, consumer products, communications, transportation, the environment, business and education have been made by people willing to be bold, take risks and envision not only the future that could be, but the future that must be.

Think about the most significant achievement of your life so far. Perhaps it is an academic accomplishment or specific success in your career. Maybe it is ultimate triumph in a test of faith such as a health or parenting crisis. Quite possibly you are the creator of a new idea, a new process or a new product. Perhaps the life of a family member or a friend is different today because you provided support or encouragement at just the right time. Regardless of the achievement, chances are that it occurred because you were bold enough to take steps that you didn't think you *could* take or *should* take or would even be *willing* to take. Your Personal Destiny is now waiting for you to take similar bold steps.

<u>Vision is compelling</u> because it has to be. People, events, ideas and products that are compelling inject themselves into your life with a riveting sense of urgency and insistence that grabs you by the shirt, pulls you up close and shouts, "Pay attention to me! I'm important!" When you feel compelled to do something, it gets done because you're absorbed in it and captivated by it. You can't imagine life any other way. You take action because you simply *must*.

Abraham Lincoln's Vision of a reunited union was compelling for him because he viewed the alternative—a shattered country—as unacceptable. His perseverance and commitment to realizing his Vision is the reason he is viewed today as one of America's greatest leaders, more than a hundred and fifty years after he was first elected. We would be quite a different country, and society, today if his Vision had not been compelling to him, and to so many others who took action to make it happen.

As I stood before the Throne and gazed up into the clouds and the dazzling sunlight that enveloped it, God spoke and once again showed me the world in the context of a massive office. Most of the chairs were empty, as they had been the first time I had viewed this scene, because the vast majority of the earth's people have still yet to discover their unique purpose on earth. But as I looked upon the office this time, I noticed that it was in a state of decay and ruin because so many people were not in the right place at the right time doing the right thing. Suddenly I became aware of the compelling nature of the earthbound Personal Destiny that God has given me, and of the equally compelling nature of the Destinies that await each of you. We each have unique roles to play, and the stakes are high for everyone else if we leave life without having fulfilled our purpose for being here. Others who need what you have to give will never receive it. God's plan for humanity on earth will be missing the piece on which your name is written. So much will be lost forever unless your Vision is compelling enough to make you—and others—take action now.

<u>Vision is inspiring</u> because it has to be. When Vision is compelling, you know you *must* respond; when Vision is inspirational, you're motivated to respond because you *want* to. Your Vision arouses emotions in you that you may not have even known that you had. Those emotions transform your spirit, awakening unknown passion that moves you to action. Your Vision must be inspiring in order to stir the same degree of commitment in others that it does in you. Since your Life Mission is unique, no one else will have the same perspective on it that you have, yet you must inspire interest in others since few of us will be able to realize our Vision and fulfill our earthbound Destiny singlehandedly.

When I was growing up in the late 1950's and early 1960's, much of our nation was captivated by the notion of traveling in space and exploring new frontiers. Kids daydreamed about being astronauts and there was an intensified interest in science and all things space. Television shows and movies began to take us into space and in 1960 we elected a president who shared an exciting vision with America in an inspiring speech two years later: landing a man on the moon by the end of the decade. We were all inspired and bought into the President's Vision with budget dollars and education and massive amounts of public support. Sure enough, on a July day in 1969—a mere five months before the arbitrary deadline—Neil Armstrong set foot on the moon and the Vision was realized largely because it had inspired so much support.

Perhaps you don't see yourself as inspiring, but there have probably been times during your life when you were. Think for a moment. When you're passionate about a belief or an idea or a product or a television show or a candidate for public office, you often find yourself recommending those things to friends, co-workers and family. But you don't just stop with a recommendation. You tell them *why* you think they should watch the show or use the product or vote for the candidate. You make a case, and you tie that case to things you already know about them . . . to ideals they hold, to concepts they find reasonable, to outcomes they like or support. Your enthusiasm inspires them to take action. Your Vision should do the same.

<u>Vision is radical</u> because it should be. Bold thinkers do things others have contemplated, and then dismissed as impossible. Radical thinkers envision a future that no else has even contemplated, let alone dismissed as impossible. They're revolutionaries who disrupt Life in unforeseen, ground-breaking fashion. Your Vision has to be disruptive or it will be lost in the clutter of today's insanely busy world. Rising above that clutter is critical because you have something special to offer the world and they need to know about it. Make a statement! Be audacious and profound and offer exhilarating change that stirs souls!

Radical thinking created the Peace Corps in the early 1960's. Although you may not think that helping chronically poor people in Third World countries is radical, consider the Vision that drove President Kennedy to create the Peace Corps. He was challenging the conventional notion that there will always be people in the world who are poor and uneducated, that those people are destined to live lives without meaning and that their situation is a problem that is simply too large for the rest of us to tackle.

Although it is true that there are still millions of poor, uneducated people in the world, it is also true that thousands of lives around the globe have been changed for the better. Poverty has been around for a long time and it will not go quietly. Yet, for radical thinkers, that is a challenge and it is challenge that drives them. They specialize in the impossible and the unheard of.

When have *you* been a radical thinker? Has there been a time in your life when you refused to accept the status quo? A time when someone told you that you couldn't accomplish something and that made you all the more determined to find some way to do it? A time when your disruptive behavior resulted in something positive? Your Personal Destiny is waiting for you to rise above the clutter of Life and break new ground in the lives of others.

<u>Vision is</u> often <u>embarrassing</u>. But if your Destiny is not something illegal, immoral or unethical, then why would you be embarrassed? Looking back on your life, there were no doubt several times you wanted to tell friends or family about something you really wanted to do or to accomplish, but you held back because of the response you expected from them . . . that your goal or dream was something you could never possibly achieve. Right? You believed that—even though they might not tell you directly—they wouldn't think that you were smart enough, strong enough, rich enough, well-connected enough or savvy enough to achieve your goal.

Sometimes, when you *did* reveal a secret passion or goal, you discovered people who *did* tell you directly. They ridiculed some or all of your Vision and questioned your sanity or your judgment for choosing the path you wanted to take. Perhaps they even sought to derail or destroy what you wanted to accomplish. So you chose not to reveal yourself anymore, abandoned your Vision and chose not to dream anymore.

Fulfilling a Personal Destiny is not for the timid or the faint of heart because it is rarely an easy path. Pressing on in the face of those obstacles requires a Vision that is confident, self-assured and tenacious. Embarrassment must be left in the dust, visible only in your rear view mirror.

As I've already told you earlier in this book, I wanted to be president of the United States for the first thirty-five years of my life. Telling *anyone* about that dream was embarrassing, with a capital "E." I got "the look" whenever I shared my dream . . .

you know, the look that says, "This is Rockford, Illinois. Nobody famous *ever* came from here, and you think *you* will be the first?!" Nobody famous, of course, except for presidential candidate John B. Anderson, Olympic skating medalist Janet Lynn, actors Aidan Quinn, Barbara Hale and Susan Saint James, rock band Cheap Trick, astronaut Janice Voss, Destiny's Child singer Michelle Williams, Secretary of Labor Lynn Martin, Jodi Benson (voice of The Little Mermaid), suffragette Julia Lathrop, Chicago Cubs catcher Ken Rudolph, billiards legend Dallas West and a host of other actors, professional athletes, business leaders, politicians and miscellaneous famous names too numerous to mention here.

All of those people were once just ordinary humans, plodding through life in Rockford, unknown to the rest of the world. Very ordinary and very unknown. In fact, in the 1930's while a high school student, Barbara Hale actually babysat my mother, years before she became known to millions on television as Perry Mason's secretary, Della Street. One of my classmates at Guilford High School, Debi Bowen, is now known as Debra Bowen. Living two thousand miles from her Rockford hometown, she is now California's Secretary of State and possibly the state's next governor and a potential candidate for national office. Passing her in the halls back in the early '70's, I would never have guessed what her future held.

All of these ordinary, once-unknown human beings have one thing in common. They each had a Destiny that was probably a bit embarrassing when they first shared it with others, though not embarrassing enough to deter them from pursuing their Vision and making a difference in the world.

Finally, Vision is measurable and specific because it simply has to be. You can't assess your progress if you're not sure where you're headed and you won't recognize your *Ultimate Destination* once you do arrive there if you don't know what it looks like. Your Vision should be filled with dates and numbers and specifics so that anyone who reads it (particularly *you*) has a clear picture of what you're going to accomplish, the dates by which you intend to have it accomplished, and the impact that it will have on the world.

It's time to develop your own Vision. Before you write, close your eyes. Think about what makes you unique and about how you can use that uniqueness to change the world, even if in only one small way. Think about the ways in which you enjoy helping people . . . teaching them, engaging with them, providing for them, mentoring them, inspiring them, encouraging them, listening to them, sharing your passion with them, loving them or being a catalyst for change in their lives.

What one thing in your life has most exhilarated or energized you? What are you most passionate about? What one thing in your life has most inspired you? What one word best describes the contribution you want to make to the world before you die?

Keep your eyes closed. Focus on your Personal Destiny, as you've just discovered it. Imagine what the world actually looks like when you *fulfill* that purpose. How do the lives of individual people change? How does our way of life as a society change? In what ways does *your* life change? Visualize it. Internalize it. See it. Touch it. Hear it. Smell it. Taste it.

Now begin to write. Five years from today, how has your Life Mission shaped what is happening in your life? In what specific ways are you fulfilling your Destiny? What is the ultimate impact on the world? Begin your Vision paragraph with a date. I chose December 31, 2018 because it is five years from the time this book was published. Write in the present tense and avoid tentative words like *try, hope, aspire, attempt, aim, strive, anticipate, expect, want, seek* and others like them. Instead, describe your Vision in terms that are certain and definite. Begin the sentences in your Vision paragraph with words like "I *am* doing . . ." or "My work *is* achieving . . ." Give yourself—and anyone else who reads your Vision—a clear picture of what life is like for you, and for the world, when your Destiny is fulfilled.

Once again, if you'd like an example to follow, allow me to share my Vision with you. As you may remember, my Life Mission is that *I exist to inspire and prepare ordinary people in all walks of Life to accomplish extraordinary things through discovering, and fulfilling, their own unique Personal Destinies.* Reflecting on that, I wrote this five-sentence Vision:

> By December 31, 2018, I speak in a different house of worship somewhere in the world every single worship day. *Undiscovered Horizons* has been translated into 30 languages and is available online and in retail stores worldwide, and 50% of those who buy the book contact me to report that they have become actively engaged in the search for—and fulfillment of—their Destiny. My Destiny blog is read every week by 50 million people around the globe, and I host an annual Destiny weekend on every continent, drawing 50,000 people to each event. *Undiscovered Horizons* coaches are coaching 25,000 people worldwide and another 100,000 attend Destiny workshops around the world. 100% of those attending these events and participating in coaching are actively engaged in the search for—and fulfillment of—their Destiny. Each week, I am invited to appear on at least one talk show or news program in the secular mainstream media that has a national, regional or large market audience, and have attracted attention and criticism in the media from atheists and others who do not believe in Divine Destiny.

You might wonder why this Vision contains so many "I" and "my" words when Destiny is <u>always</u> about glorifying God and serving others. This is because realizing your Vision can only occur when you use your unique set of divinely gifted skills, abilities and talents to create experiences for others that enable them to arrive at the Ultimate Destination (fulfillment of your Personal Destiny) right alongside you. When that happens, the world changes in the way in which God intended.

So, I also wrote a second paragraph that describes what the Ultimate Destination looks like when I arrive there, having realized my Vision. I did this to remind myself (and anyone who reads my

Vision) that although I'm a key player in my Vision, fulfillment of my Destiny is all about how the lives of others are impacted and changed. This is how I see the world as my Destiny continues to be fulfilled, ten years from now:

> On December 31, 2023, Divine Destiny is an ongoing topic of debate in the mainstream media worldwide. Increasing numbers of people worldwide believe in Divine Destiny and seek to discover and fulfill it. As Destiny becomes real for more and more people, crime, war, political discord, divorce, incivility and depression become visibly, and measurably—less prevalent. Levels of charitable giving and volunteerism increase significantly over prior years as well.

The first thing you'll notice is that I've violated one of the rules to which Vision statements must conform. The elements of this paragraph are not measurable. For example, I say that Devine Destiny is an ongoing topic of debate, yet offer no benchmark that defines how we know when it has achieved that status. I talk about "increasing numbers of people" without identifying those numbers or defining a specific rate of growth. I mention the decline of various social and societal ills without citing any numbers that would quantify (and prove) such a decline. Likewise, increases in charitable giving and volunteerism are also not quantified.

Actually, I wrote this particular Vision in this manner on purpose. I wanted you to see how much less compelling a Vision is when it is not measurable and the visionary is, therefore, not held accountable for specific results. I will never know when, or if, I've achieved this Vision unless I include specific thresholds in it that define success in real terms. Vision must be a collection of measurable elements if we are to ever know that it has been realized. I have some more work to do.

Once you've written a Vision that characterizes the state of your Life Mission at a specific point in the future and another that describes arrival at your *Ultimate Destination* (fulfillment of your Personal Destiny), re-read them. Do they originate in your heart, and in the farthest reaches of your imagination? Are they unique to you? Bold and compelling? Perhaps a bit embarrassing? Measurable? If your answers are consistently "Yes," then your Vision of the achievement of your Life Mission, and your Vision of the fulfillment of your Personal Destiny, are ready to pursue.

I'd like to know where you're headed so that I can offer support and encouragement to you. Once both of your Vision statements are "ready," please share them with me at JimMcComb@UndiscoveredHorizons.com.

Appendix C
Success Measures

Success Measures (Goals)

Success measures are calculable outcome measures of the progress you're making (goals you're achieving) toward the fulfillment of your earthbound Personal Destiny. These measures should be ones for which you can physically see progress. You should know objectively whether or not they have been achieved. Measures are important because without them it is impossible to quantify the difference you're making in the world, and quantifying that difference is important because measurable progress keeps you motivated and focused. When others see visible progress, they're more likely to support your journey and to walk along with you.

Success measures assess what is critically important to the fulfillment of your Personal Destiny. They assess outcomes rather than the activities that lead to those outcomes. For example, writing this book is fundamental to my Destiny. A proper Success Measure would be the percentage of those buying this book that actually identifies their Destiny, works actively to fulfill it and communicates with me to verify that activity. Simply measuring the number of books sold does nothing to define the actual change in the world that will come from people actually reading the book and taking action. Be careful not to focus on activities or you will lose sight of the real outcomes that will bring fulfillment of your Destiny.

Every Success Measure:

- Is clear and specific
- Measures progress made toward fulfilling a specific part of your Vision
- Defines progress through a specific, desired computable result
- Includes annual "checkpoint results" that show measured progress toward the ultimate achievement of the desired result
- Includes a final deadline by which the desired result will ultimately be achieved
- Must have an owner, a specific person responsible for seeing that the desired result is achieved by the desired deadline

One of the key Success Measures found in the Vision that I shared with you on page 172 is that 50% of the people who read *Undiscovered Horizons* will contact me and let me know that they're using this book to engage actively in a search for their earthbound Personal Destiny and in the fulfillment of that Destiny. This measure meets all of the tests listed above. It is clear and specific and is a definite measure of whether or not my Vision is having an impact on the world. Since my email address appears regularly in this book, I am the owner of this measure and the deadline is the date that appears in my Vision. Checkpoint results don't appear directly in the Vision, but I have defined them for year-end 2013, 2014, 2015, 2016 and 2017 and those numbers appear in my personal plan. The *Undiscovered Horizons Personal Destiny Plan* workbook has a place to record your checkpoint results.

As you begin to develop your Success Measures, start by reviewing your Vision because it is in that paragraph that success (fulfillment . . . your *Ultimate Destination*) for your life is defined. First, identify the individual elements, or components, of your Vision. As an example, these are some of the elements in the Vision that I shared with you on page 172:

- I speak in a different house of worship somewhere in the world each worship day
- *Undiscovered Horizons* has been translated into 30 languages
- 100,000 people attend Destiny workshops worldwide each year

Look at each sentence in your Vision and identify and list all of the elements that exist in each sentence. These elements define your ultimate success and should be quantifiable outcomes that move you toward fulfillment of your Destiny.

In order to avoid tackling a Destiny that is beyond the scope of your time, money and energy, try to keep your Vision elements (and, therefore, your Success Measures) to no more than a dozen. Set your Vision date at least three years from now. Five years or ten years into the future are other dates you might use as targets for Destiny fulfillment. The date you select will depend on the scope of your Destiny and may also depend on your age. For example, I'm almost 59 as I write this sentence; anything beyond a twenty-year fulfillment is probably unreasonable for me, even given the advancing life expectancies of Americans these days.

What kinds of Success Measures should exist in your Vision? We've already discussed Time. Your Vision should always begin with the date in the future by which you have fulfilled (or have made *significant* progress fulfilling) your earthbound Personal Destiny. Contemplate the scope of your Destiny. Ask God for direction in what He wants you to accomplish and how long that might take. Select a date that you feel led to work toward.

The date you select is a deadline, although not necessarily one that is cast in stone. As circumstances change, both in your own life and out in the world, you may want to adjust that deadline at some point in the future. Just don't use your ability to adjust your deadline as an excuse for a lack of diligence and commitment in fulfilling your Destiny.

Other Success Measures that may be a part of your Vision include:

- Frequency (such as my *annual* Destiny Weekends)
- Growth (for example, an *X% increase* in awareness by a certain group of people about a particular topic)
- Perception (such as *50%* of the readers of this book being *inspired* enough by its message to actively *engage* in a search for their own Destiny)
- Quality (for example, the *average rating* you receive from audiences at speeches you give or participants in any workshops you do)
- Quantity as measured by numbers or ratios (for example, the *number* of people who have enrolled in an online membership community you have set up, or the *percentage* of people who now have a certain attribute because of you)
- Reward (for example, a specific benefit realized by your target audience, such as *time* saved, *knowledge* learned or *dollars* earned)

Remember to define some annual "checkpoint results" for each of your Success Measures so that you can gradually work up to the Success Measures stated in your Vision. The checkpoint results, as well as your ultimate Success Measures, should be realistic, stretch targets that you are deeply committed to achieving.

Once you've identified the Success Measures in your Vision, refined them if necessary, defined checkpoint results for them and ensured that they have all of the attributes listed at the top of page 176, send them to me at JimMcComb@UndiscoveredHorizons.com. I'd love to follow your progress, right along with you!

Appendix D

Strategies

Strategies (Life's Most Incredible Odyssey)

Strategies are paths of action that collectively contribute to the realization of your Vision. They are based on your Success Measures and are generally expressed as proactive statements describing the approach to achieving the various outcomes that are inherent in your Vision. The strategies you ultimately choose are important because they become the key priorities around which you allocate your time, money, energy, ideas and other assets.

Before developing your strategies, take stock of the ways in which both you and your environment impact your Vision. The business world calls this an environmental scan, and formerly called it a SWOT analysis, with the letters representing Strengths, Weaknesses, Opportunities and Threats. Strengths and weaknesses are *internal*. You generally have complete control over them, and they occur *because* of things that you think or say or do. Opportunities and threats are *external*. They are issues and events over which you have little or no control, and they usually occur *in spite* of things that you think or say or do. Strengths and opportunities create advantages in your life that become catalysts for more effectively fulfilling your Personal Destiny. On the other hand, weaknesses and threats create disadvantages in your life that become the roadblocks that prevent you from effectively fulfilling that Destiny.

Formulating strategy requires that you have a clear understanding of what it will take to achieve the end result (the Success Measure) for which you're developing the strategy. You also need to fully comprehend the impact that your personal strengths, weaknesses, opportunities and threats will have on the path that you take to achieve that end result.

So, begin by listing the Success Measures in your Vision. For my Vision, which I shared with you on page 172, the list looks like this:

- Speak in a different house of worship somewhere in the world every single worship day
- *Undiscovered Horizons* has been translated into 30 languages
- *Undiscovered Horizons* is available online and in retail stores worldwide
- 50% of those who buy the book contact me to report that they have become actively engaged in the search for—and fulfillment of—their Destiny
- Destiny blog read every week by 50 million people around the globe
- Annual Destiny weekend on every continent, drawing 50,000 people to each event
- *Undiscovered Horizons* coaches are coaching 25,000 people worldwide
- 100,000 people attend Destiny workshops around the world
- 100% of those participating in the coaching and the workshops are actively engaged in the search for—and fulfillment of—their Destiny

- Each week, I am invited to appear on at least one talk show or news program in the secular mainstream media that has a national, regional or large market audience
- My message has attracted attention and criticism in the media from atheists and others who do not believe in Divine Destiny

Now think about the things you must do to achieve the outcomes of each of *your* Success Measures. What collective set of action steps will take you to each outcome? Are those steps consistent with your Life Mission and your core values? In what ways will your path to each outcome be influenced by your strengths and opportunities? How must you leverage and exploit them in order to more easily or more effectively realize your Vision? In what ways will your path to each outcome be influenced by your strengths and opportunities? How must you mitigate, neutralize, or even eliminate them in order to more easily or more effectively realize your Vision? Do you have the knowledge, skills, passion and capacity necessary to achieve each outcome?

As you contemplate the answers to these questions, the paths to each of your outcomes (Success Measures) will begin to become clearer in your mind. For each of your outcomes, jot down a sentence that expresses the path that will take you there. Make it a complete sentence that includes an action verb. The *Undiscovered Horizons Personal Destiny Plan* workbook provides templates for your use in developing your Strategies, although you can certainly use a blank piece of paper as well.

Once you have written your path (Strategy) for achieving each of your outcomes, look at your entire list of outcomes and circle those that you think are the most critical to the achievement of your overall Vision. Which of them form the very foundation of your Vision? Which of those outcomes, if achieved, will bring about the accomplishment of some of your other Success Measures?

For example, as I looked at the rather lengthy list of Success Measures in my own Vision, four of them jumped out at me as critical to the overall fulfillment of my Vision and, therefore, my earthbound Personal Destiny:

- Speak in a different house of worship somewhere in the world every single worship day
- *Undiscovered Horizons* is available online and in retail stores worldwide
- 50% of those who buy the book contact me to report that they have become actively engaged in the search for—and fulfillment of—their Destiny
- Each week, I am invited to appear on at least one talk show or news program in the secular mainstream media that has a national, regional or large market audience

I chose these four based on this line of reasoning: If I am ever to fulfill my Destiny—to help you and others find and fulfill your Destinies—then you all must necessarily be exposed to the message I was given in Heaven so you can determine how it applies to your own life. This means that both the faith-based and secular communities in the world must have an opportunity to hear me talk about it, and have an opportunity to obtain a copy of *Undiscovered Horizons*. But exposure to the message is only the beginning; fulfillment of my Destiny can only come when you receive and act on it.

These four outcomes, in my opinion, will also lead to the accomplishment of the other eight Success Measures in my Vision. If enough people are exposed to my message during speaking engagements and media interviews, and are moved enough by that message to seek out a copy of *Undiscovered Horizons*, then the book will get into the hands of a significant portion of the population, provided it is readily available online and in bookstores. If the book becomes a bestseller, and at least half of those who buy it are moved enough by my message to take action, then the outcomes around coaching, blog readership, workshops and the Destiny weekends will have a chance to be realized. If enough people in other countries are moved to action by the message, translations are bound to occur and if the message receives enough attention from the media it is inevitable that opponents will surface and their criticism will generate the debate that will make Devine Destiny a mainstream topic of discussion.

Once you've chosen your key outcomes, look for the synergies they have with the other Success Measures in your Vision to ensure that the ones you chose are truly the foundation on which your Vision is built.

Narrowing the twelve outcomes in my Vision down to just four is important because Life is about priorities. There is never enough time, money, energy, bandwidth, etc. for us to do everything we need to do at any given moment. So we must prioritize. The experts who know about such things tell us that a normal human being can generally focus on achieving no more than a half dozen goals or projects during a particular time period. For our purposes here, let's define that time period as a year.

So, narrow the outcomes (Success Measures) in your own Vision down to the six (or fewer) that, once achieved, will help you make the greatest possible amount of progress toward fulfilling your Vision and, therefore, your Destiny. Since you've already drafted a Strategy for each of them, you now have the strategic priorities for your life (and your Destiny) for the next year.

Because the elements of your SWOT analysis, particularly the opportunities and threats, will evolve and change over time, you should plan to re-evaluate them each year. While Life Mission, Vision and Success Measures are unlikely to change much over time, your Strategies (and the Tactics we will discuss in the next section) will be affected by the changes in your strengths, weaknesses, opportunities and threats. As a result, your Strategies are likely to change every year so you should be prepared to revise them as needed. As you adjust your Strategies, you may find that your priorities will change as well. That is normal and natural.

Now that you've defined Strategies for each of your Success Measures, prioritized them, and selected the highest priorities to focus on during the coming year, review them and ask yourself a couple of pertinent questions. Is the Strategy you've written for each outcome (Success Measure) in your Vision the most clear and direct path to achieve that outcome? Are the Strategies you chose as the highest priorities on which to focus for the year ahead clearly the Strategies that will help you make the most significant—and most immediate—progress toward fulfilling your Vision? If so, they're ready for prime time! Please send them to me at JimMcComb@UndiscoveredHorizons.com, as I would welcome a chance to see where you'll be headed in the next twelve months.

Appendix E

Tactics

Tactics (Destiny Action Steps)

Tactics are the action steps that you take along the paths (Strategies) that lead to the fulfillment of your Vision and, therefore, your earthbound Personal Destiny. Completed Tactics mean a fulfilled Destiny. Each of your Strategies will have at least one action step, and usually more than one. Completing some action steps actually prompts the addition of new tactics to your to-do list, while others are added simply because you didn't think of them when you initially developed your Destiny Plan.

Tactics include a clear statement of the <u>exact action to be taken</u>, a specific <u>timeframe</u> within which the action will be taken or a <u>deadline</u> by which it will be completed (put all beginning and ending dates on your personal calendar so that your Tactics will become a part of your day-to-day to-do list), the name of the person (usually your name, but occasionally a family member or personal advisor) who has ultimate <u>accountability</u> for completing the action step, and any hard cost (<u>cash outlay or tangible resource</u>) or soft cost (<u>time or intangible resource</u>) necessary to complete it.

Each strategy will have at least one action step (Tactic), and will generally have several, depending on how complex the Strategy is. List your action steps in chronological order in your Destiny Plan, according to the dates you need to begin working on them. This establishes a logical flow of action for each Strategy, and is better than listing actions by deadlines because beginning an action step on time ensures that you'll never be caught by surprise because your personal calendar only tells you deadlines. Ideally, you should transfer *every* action step date—starting point, progress dates along the way and deadline—to your personal calendar so that your action steps become a part of your everyday to-do list and are completed on time.

Think about your priority Strategies. Visualize each of them a separate path leading to the fulfillment of your earthbound Personal Destiny. Visualize each of them as an actual path, much like a hiking trail you might follow through a national park or up the base of a mountain as you prepare to climb it. As you travel such a path, you put one foot in front of the other. Your steps are calculated and deliberate, so you don't stumble. Your steps are logical, so they keep you moving forward on the path toward your destination. You're conscious of time because you don't want to be on the path after dark. You brought supplies . . . food, water, matches, a warm coat and a first-aid kit (maybe even a flashlight!) . . . because you want to be prepared for anything that might happen along the way. Just as a day hike needs to be planned to ensure a desired result, the action steps along any strategic path must be planned as well.

Before putting pen to paper, ask yourself what action you should be taking in the next year in order to ensure that you realize your Vision by the date you set. In what way does your life need to change? What do you need to do differently tomorrow than you did yesterday?

The first step in writing your Tactics is to note the major activities that would accomplish each Strategy. There is no magic number here. I generally have three or four major activities for each of my strategies, but yours may vary. Some will have more than three major activities, and some will have fewer than that.

The second step in writing Tactics is to determine the steps that will accomplish each major activity. What information do you need to gather? Who do you need to contact, and why? What documents or materials need to be created? These various "needs" led to the action steps that I created as I contemplated how to meet those needs. What "needs" will help you accomplish the major activities within each of your Strategies? How will you meet those "needs?" Your answers to these questions will provide you with your Tactics (action steps).

Drop me a line at JimMcComb@UndiscoveredHorizons.com. and let me take a look at your Tactics. I'd love to see how you'll be traveling each of your Strategic paths during the year ahead!

Appendix F

Evaluating Progress

Evaluating Progress (Destiny Evolution)

As you go about the day-by-day, month-by-month and year-by-year activities that will collectively contribute to the fulfillment of your earthbound Personal Destiny, you will find that your progress is not occurring as quickly as you had hoped. Or perhaps your progress will be detoured by events that occur in the world, or more specifically in your personal life. As a result, you'll often find yourself taking corrective action as you continually evaluate the progress you're making toward your *Ultimate Destination*.

For example, you might add to, adjust, or even delete some of your Strategies. Your Tactics will be in a constant state of flux as you complete them while others are springing up to take their place. It is even possible that Life may throw you a significant curve ball and one or two of the Success Measures in your Vision may need to be changed. This is all simply a part of the inevitable evolution of your Destiny, and you should never view corrective action as a sign that you have failed, or that you have strayed off course. God's purpose for your life on earth never changes, even though the path to achieve that purpose occasionally changes. Remember that, and take comfort in it.

Once your Destiny Plan is completed and you have begun the journey toward the *Ultimate Destination* that is the fulfillment of your Destiny, you should find a quiet corner once a month and sit down with your Success Measures, Strategies, and Tactics. Ask these questions:

> Am I missing any of the deadlines I set for the accomplishment of any of my Tactics or Strategies? If so, why I am I missing deadlines? Is it because of issues that are under my control, such as lack of motivation and diligence or poor time management? Is it because of issues beyond my control, such as new job responsibilities at work or the need to care for an ill child or spouse?

> Are the deadlines I set realistic, or are they too ambitious? Do I need to re-set any of them? If so, can I be sure that I'm choosing the right deadlines this time so I don't have to re-set them again?

> Are my Success Measures the right ones by which to measure success in my Vision, or do I need to make an adjustment somewhere? Why or why not?

> Should any of my Success Measures be eliminated because they are no longer relevant? If so, why? Should any of them simply be replaced with a new or revised Success Measure? Why or why not?

> Have any of my Strategies or Tactics been completed? Are any of them now obsolete for any reason? Do they need to be updated, or replaced altogether with new Strategies or Tactics? Why or why not?

Is my Vision (Personal Destiny) still an appropriate future destination for my Life Mission (purpose), or do I need to adjust my Vision in some way? Why or why not?

Essentially, the bottom line of evaluating your progress on a regular basis is to determine whether or not you're on track to fulfill your earthbound Personal Destiny within the parameters you've set for yourself. If you're not on track, this is the point at which you determine why you're not and what you plan to do about it. Most months, though, you'll find yourself generally where you're supposed to be and no corrective action will be needed.

If you do find yourself off course and need a little boost getting back on track, drop me a note at JimMcComb@UndiscoveredHorizons.com. I'm happy to give you a hand. If you *are* on track, take a moment to celebrate your success! Then take another moment and email me; I'd like to share that success moment with you!

Lightning Source UK Ltd.
Milton Keynes UK
UKOW02n2049210816

281132UK00001B/5/P